Thomas Henry Farrer

The State in It's Relation to Trade

Thomas Henry Farrer

The State in It's Relation to Trade

ISBN/EAN: 9783744725927

Printed in Europe, USA, Canada, Australia, Japan

Cover: Foto ©ninafisch / pixelio.de

More available books at **www.hansebooks.com**

THE STATE

IN ITS

RELATION TO TRADE

BY

T. H. FARRER

London

MACMILLAN AND CO.

1883

PREFACE.

WHEN first asked to write on the Relations of the State to Trade, I saw with pleasure that Mr. Stanley Jevons was to write on the Relations of the State to Labour, and hoped that we might consult with one another on the line to be taken and on the distinction to be made between these two kindred subjects. For some time circumstances prevented me from writing, and when I was able to do so, his treatise had appeared, and he, alas! was prematurely lost to us. In the following pages I have tried to avoid the ground which he has occupied; but find the tendency of my own opinions on one point slightly diverging from his. It is not difficult to account for this. He knew much more of local government and of local wants than I do; I perhaps have seen more of the difficulties and weakness of central government than he had; the general impression left on my mind is therefore rather more adverse to central state interference than his was. In thus referring to

Mr. Jevons I can only add to the many public expressions of regret for his loss my own tribute of sincere admiration for one to whom we owed so much and from whom we expected so much more; one who as a statistician had the rare faculty of using figures with intelligence and discrimination; one who as an economist treated society not as a machine, subject to dead mechanical rules, but as a living, growing, changing organism; one, above all, who in whatever he did was a sincere lover of truth and of his fellow-men.

TABLE OF CONTENTS.

CONTENTS.

CHAPTER X.

CHAPTER XI.

CHAPTER XII.

CHAPTER XIII.

CHAPTER XVIII.

CHAPTER XIX.

CHAPTER XX.

STATE IN ITS RELATION TO TRADE.

CHAPTER I.

WHAT IS THE MEANING OF THE STATE AND OF TRADE?

WHEN we speak of the state in its relation to trade, the questions at once arise, what do we mean by the state, and what do we mean by the trade, of England? It will be well to answer the second of these questions first, for it is not till we know what is the subject with which the state has relations that we can put a meaning on the somewhat vague entity which has relations with it, or on the nature of those relations.

Meaning of Trade.—Taken in its widest sense, trade may be held to include all operations by which skill and labour, and the products of skill and labour, are exchanged—the hiring of the workman, and the employment of the professional man, as well as the buying and selling of material wares. But I am relieved from travelling over so wide a field by the treatise which Mr. Stanley Jevons has contributed to this series on the subject of the relation of the state to labour, and I shall therefore, as far as possible,

B

avoid touching upon the many points in which the state comes in contact with the employment and hire of personal labour and skill.

The field remaining to me is only too wide for adequate discussion in a treatise of this kind. It comprises all buying and selling of material commodities or material services, and all the subsidiary operations of capital and credit; of capital, which is the title to existing material commodities; of credit, which is the trust that material commodities will be forthcoming: *Quidquid emunt homines nostri est farrago libelli.*

The trade of this country is a very large and a very varied thing. There is, in the first place, all the buying and selling which goes on within the country itself: every village shop, every cooperative store, every market, every dealing between retailers, merchants, manufacturers, importers, and producers; every banking and financial establishment in the United Kingdom; with all the subsidiary elements of agency, of brokerage, and of carriage, which are necessary for their operations. But of these internal operations, vast as they are, we have no complete measure in figures. The aggregate value of our home trade is not given in any official statistics; and of the different attempts which have been made to estimate it, none appear to me to be trustworthy; we have no complete returns of all our home industries; and even if we had, it would be almost impossible to distinguish how much of those industries and their profits is due to foreign, and how much to home, markets. But our ultimate consumption at home of articles produced, or partly produced, at home, must be enormous, and the home trade which supplies that consumption must be enormous also. The causes of our immense internal trade are to be found in our great accumulated wealth; in the differences of rank, class, and occupation, producing an immense variety of wants; in the variety as well as the mass of things which the country produces; in the coal and iron which enable us to manufacture; above all, in the energy, skill, and ambition of our people, in their desire to improve their condition, and the facilities which their own character and their free institutions give them for so doing.

We are also the greatest of traders with other nations. The exports and imports of the United Kingdom are estimated to be nearly one-fourth of the foreign trade of the whole world; and if the trade carried on with English capital between foreign countries were included, our foreign trade would be found to amount to much more.

We are also the greatest capitalists, the largest lenders to foreign nations; and we reap the benefit in that excess of imports which is so much dreaded by protectionists and fair traders. Good statisticians estimate our investments abroad at not much less than £2,000,000,000.

We are the greatest of brokers; we do the business of agents for other nations, and we get an ample commission upon it.

We are the greatest of carriers. Our shipping—ever growing, both actually and also proportionately to that of other nations—is now equal to more than one-half of the shipping of the whole world. The value of our ships is estimated to exceed £100,000,000; the amount of cargoes afloat under our flag at any given moment is very much larger; and the property covered by

it in the course of a year is probably not less than
£1,000,000,000. Our ocean trade is two-thirds or more
of the ocean trade of the whole world. Our superiority
in shipping is due, in part, to the causes I have mentioned above, but also and especially to the courage
and seamanship of our mariners, and to the skill of
our engineers.

It would be easy to illustrate the magnitude of our
foreign trade by further details. But I will not
attempt to give figures which are easily accessible
in the *Statistical Abstract*, and other well known
compilations.

Meaning of the State.—The essential feature of trade,
in other words, of buying and selling, consists in a free
exchange of commodities between two persons; each
giving to the other something which he wants less and
the other wants more than the thing which the other
gives to him; and the exchange may be either completed
at once or may be the subject of a mutual promise or
contract. In one sense every thing which lies outside
this free dealing between the two persons concerned may
be called the state. Every dealing is surrounded and
limited by a large number of circumstances which are independent of the will of the parties; and every dealing may
involve a large series of consequences which the parties
themselves do not, and often cannot, provide for. Besides
positive law, there are customs and habits, either of the
whole community, or of particular classes, which individual buyers and sellers can no more disregard than they
can disregard the law itself—customs and habits which
are often only law in process of formation. We feel the
support or the weight (as it may be) of these habits in
almost every action of our lives; and as they proceed from

the instincts or desires of the community, whether expressed and conscious, or silent and unconscious, we
might possibly include these under the term "state."
But to do so would lead us too far, and we must reject
all that lies outside of, and restricts freedom of buying
and selling, as beyond our proper scope, unless it is
embodied in positive rules which can be enforced.

This limitation however, still leaves us a very large
field.   There remains the whole domain in which the
state, acting through the means of law and administration, which are the expressed voice of the state, affects
buying and selling.   It does so in a variety of ways.
It affords security ; it enforces and limits contracts ; it
regulates monopolies; it places restrictions on certain
dealings.   In some cases, and those the most extensive,
its function is to render trade practicable and to facili-
tate its operations : in other cases its function is in the
nature of interference with what traders might otherwise do.   To give a short outline of these functions is
the object of this treatise.

CHAPTER II.

THE ACTION OF THE STATE IS EFFECTED THROUGH THE LEGISLATURE; THE COURTS OF LAW; AND THE EXECUTIVE.

THE general action of the state is effected through various organisations.

Of these the Legislature is the most important. It is of course supreme over the rest; and, except in the case of judge-made law, which is an interpretation by the Courts of the customs of trade, or an application by them of existing legal analogies to new cases, all interference with trade originates with the Legislature. The Legislature carries its will into effect in two distinct ways. It may pass laws which give certain rights and remedies to the persons interested, and may leave it to them to enforce the law by taking their own proceedings, according to their own interests, in the courts of law. In this case the Courts are the organs through which the state exercises its power. Or, again, the Legislature may intrust the duty of enforcing the law to an executive department, which then becomes the organ of the state for the purpose. The latter is the more obvious and direct, and I believe at present the more popular, form of interference: and in many cases it is necessary.

But when the other form of interference is practicable, it is probably the more searching and effective, and it is free from the numerous objections which exist to the creation of hosts of inspectors and officials. What people do not see is that the two forms of interference are generally incompatible. There may be a remedy by way of penalty or damages; or there may be a remedy by way of government supervision, but there cannot be both. If a government officer has stated an article to be what it pretends to be, or what free contract or the law requires it to be, no purchaser can refuse to receive it or recover damages for loss which he sustains by its defects. If a government inspector has certified a mine, or a ship, or a railway, or a house to be safe, the mine owner, the ship owner, the railway company, or the builder are freed from all liability, civil or criminal, in courts of law, on the ground that it was unsafe, however unsafe it may really be, and however culpable the conduct which made it unsafe.

The two forms of interference are sometimes contrasted as "Prevention" and "Cure"; and it is said that prevention is better than cure. It is better, say the advocates of government supervision, to prevent a wrong being done, than to punish it or give damages for it when done. But the contrast is false. A remedy which inflicts a heavy punishment, whether in the shape of imprisonment or damages, for an injury, is a deterrent as effective as—often more effective than—the presence of a policeman. "You are hanged," said the judge to the criminal, "not because you committed murder, but in order that other persons, when tempted, may not commit murder." On the other hand, there are many cases in which there is great difficulty in bringing home a criminal remedy, or even a remedy in damages. But the question between the direct interference of a government and the remedy by penalty or damages must in all cases be, not whether "prevention is better than cure," but which of the two modes of prevention is the most practicable and most effectual.

The direct interference of the executive is exercised either by one of the departments of the central government presided over by a minister of the Crown, responsible to Parliament, or by some local authority, such as the municipal council of a town. Whether exercised by the one body or the other it is equally the operation of the state; and we shall find that both the one and the other, and sometimes both, are constantly called into play according to the difference of the subject-matter. Until late years there has been some indisposition on the part of Parliament to trust large powers to local representative bodies, arising partly from interested opposition, partly from mistrust of local authorities, partly, perhaps, from a jealousy of parting with power —a feeling which actuates popular assemblies no less than kings and ministers. But there appears at present to be an increasing and wholesome feeling in favour of delegating the control of local matters to local bodies; a most desirable thing, both because it relieves the overburdened Legislature and the growing central administration; and still more because it encourages the development of public spirit and political capacity throughout the country.

The treatise by Mr. Traill on Central Government, which forms part of this series, describes the several great offices of state and their several duties. It is therefore unnecessary for me to give any general account of

the way in which the various administrative functions
of the state relating to trade are distributed amongst the
departments.   That distribution can scarcely be referred
to any general principle, since it has been a matter of
history and of accident, rather than of design ; and the
functions of government which affect trade are exercised
by different departments without much regard to logical
consistency.   Much has been said lately about a Ministry
of Commerce, but no very distinct programme of its
functions has yet been formulated.   It would no doubt
be possible to rearrange the duties of the several departments more logically than they are now arranged, and to
give to a minister for trade a higher and more definite
position in the government.   But it must be remembered
that, do what you will, the duties of such a minister must
necessarily run into and mingle with those of other
ministers ; that many of the relations of the government with trade have for their object, not trade itself,
but some other object which is the proper subject for
another department of the state ; and, above all, that
the name of the minister, and even the arrangement of
business, is of much less importance than the character,
position, and ability of the particular officers, political or
permanent, who have to do it.   If any such change as is
proposed should be made, may I be allowed to express
a hope that the time-honoured name of the "Board of
Trade" may still be preserved,—a name connected for
evil or for good with the history of our government.
our colonies, and our commerce, from the time of Oliver
Cromwell to that of Mr. Gladstone.

CHAPTER III.

THERE are certain general functions of the state which have no special relation to traders more than to any other class of the people, but without which trade could not flourish, and could scarcely exist. Such are the following :

Protection to Life and Property.—By means of the police, of the criminal law, and · of civil remedies for violence and injury, the state affords that security against robbery and wrong without which free buying and selling would come to an end. No goods could be safely carried or kept for sale without it. The cattle markets of the Scotch border would have been impracticable in the old days of cattle lifting ; and a few days of such riots as Lord George Gordon's, would stop the business of London. The robber barons of the Rhine were put down in the interests of the trading towns of Germany ; and the growth of maritime commerce has led the nations to treat pirates as the one class of criminals whom no flag protects from condign punishment.

But it is needless to illustrate this point. The first and most essential relation of the state to trade is to afford security for life and property.

Settlement of Disputes.—In establishing courts of law with the requisite powers, the state provides the means of settling the questions concerning property which arise between its subjects, and which, in a trading country like ours, are especially numerous and important. It is in the process of determining such disputes that a body of law is formed; by adopting the customs of traders as their guide, and reducing those customs to logical consistency, a succession of able judges have produced our excellent system of mercantile law. It may be added that the function of the state in settling disputes is distinguishable by no definite line from its function of enforcing contracts, which is more fully noticed below.

Education.—General education, from reading, writing, and arithmetic, upwards, is essential to business. Beyond this, the state gives a certain amount of special assistance to manufactures, by helping to establish museums, and by making grants to science and art schools. It is probable that technical education has yet to receive a much greater development in this country, and the state will no doubt be called upon to take a large part in it.

Information.—The state furnishes this in a variety of ways, many of which are generally, and some specially, concerned with trade.

It undertakes scientific observations and publications which private effort cannot accomplish. Among these are astronomical observations and the *Nautical Almanac*; hydrographic surveys and admiralty charts; surveys and maps of the United Kingdom ; geological and mining surveys and records ; magnetic and meteorological observations.   It publishes elaborate statistics of all matters coming under the cognisance of public departments, of which those relating to the foreign trade of the country are amongst the most important.   It collects, through the diplomatic and consular service, reports concerning the trade and industries of foreign countries, and it lays before the public either in the *Gazette* or in Parliamentary Papers a great variety of information on subjects connected with trade.

CHAPTER IV.

THE STATE ENFORCES, EXPLAINS, AND ADDS TO CONTRACTS.

To enforce contracts is, as we have said, one function of the state. It is a function of great importance, and is especially connected with trade. The nature of this function, therefore, calls for some general observations.

Freedom of Contract.—Every act of buying and selling, unless completely executed at once, constitutes what the lawyers call a contract. But is not contract free? Is not anybody at liberty to make or not to make a contract of purchase or sale, and, if so, is he not in so doing out of the domain of state interference? To the first of these questions I shall reply presently. To the second I say—By no means. The very notion of a promise, an obligation which the law will enforce, implies that the transaction is not complete without the sanction of law; that it is one which the law steps in to complete if either of the parties fails to do so. This is the action of the state in its most powerful and all-pervading form, so universal in its operation that we hardly think of its existence. But it could not exist among men who are not bound together by strong common institutions: it only does exist in its fully developed form in very highly organised communities. The point is an important one, and is often lost sight of. Freedom of contract is often spoken of as if it were the same as simple freedom of action or disposition. But it is no such thing.

Contract involves obligation, which is the opposite of freedom. When a man makes a contract he gives up a portion of his freedom; he binds himself by a promise to another person to do or not to do certain things; and this promise, if binding in the eye of the law, is one which society, with all its crushing and overwhelming power, will compel him to perform. To use the words of a recent book of authority, "Every person not subject to any legal incapacity may dispose freely of his actions and property within the limits allowed by the general law. Liability on a contract consists in a limitation of this disposing power by a voluntary act of the party which places some portion of that power at the command of the other party to the contract. So much of the contractor's individual freedom is taken from him and made over to the other party to the contract."[1] Freedom of contract is, therefore, a very different thing from freedom of action and disposition. So far from the doctrine of contract being identical with freedom, it is *pro tanto* the reverse. So far from its being non-interference on the part of the state with individual action, it is interference of the most subtle, searching, and overwhelming kind. It brings the whole weight of the social fabric upon the man who has bound himself by a promise. His freedom consists in being able to make or to abstain from making a binding promise. But when he has made it, the state uses its whole

[1] *Pollock on Contracts*, p. 187, 2nd ed.

despotic power to compel or prevent his free action.
Care therefore has been taken by the state to prevent
the abuse of such a power. The law of contract—a
branch of law which is ever growing in importance,
in magnitude, and in complexity—is, in fact, a statement
of the limitations which it has been found necessary to
impose on absolute freedom of contract, the definition
of the conditions under which, and of the manner in
which, a man may make such a promise as the law
will enforce.

The great difference between the system of free contract and the system which it replaced lies, not in the
absence of obligation, but in the substitution of a self-
imposed obligation for an obligation imposed by some
external power. The progress made in the last hundred
years has consisted in the abolition of a great number
of the restrictions which, whether in the form of feudal,
tribal, or family relations, of trade guilds and their
rules, or of the protective industrial systems of modern
Europe, made a large part of each man's obligation
depend, not on his own individual choice, but on certain
rules and relations laid down and determined for him
by society, by custom, and by law. The substitution of
the rights and duties arising from the free contract of
the individual for the duties arising from status and
relation is one feature in the history of that development of the individual, which in the domain of law has
been so well illustrated by Sir H. Maine, and which is
no less marked in the domains of political, of social,
and religious liberty than in that of buying and selling,
in which it has played so important a part.

In adopting freedom of contract as the general principle governing mercantile dealings, what has been done

is not to abolish obligation, but to substitute for an obligation devised by custom or law an obligation self-imposed by the individual, and this obligation, the state, not without many additions and limitations, undertakes to enforce.

Contracts Enforced by the State.—The widest and most important function of the state with relation to trade is then to enforce contracts ; and it does this by means of suits for damages and for specific performance in courts of law. In the next chapter will be found mention of some of the branches of law into which this great function of the state develops. To treat it fully is of course impossible, for to do so would be to write a treatise on mercantile law, to enume-rate all the legal rules which affect both retail and wholesale dealings.

I have said that in enforcing self-imposed obligations the state does so with many limitations and also with many additions. Of the limitations I shall speak below. On the additions it may be desirable to add a few general observations, so as to show how much the state does, not only in enforcing the actual obligations which people have made for themselves, but in so construing those obligations as to make them in many cases far more extensive than the parties ever really con-templated.

Contracts Explained and Supplemented by the State.— The great principle which governs the action of the law, *i.e.* the action of the state, in these cases, is that free and intelligent consent is of the essence of such a contract as the law will enforce. This is entirely at one with the economical principle which relies on free and intelligent choice, dictated by self-interest, as the most efficient agent in the production of wealth. In cases where there is no such free and intelligent consent, no such free choice, the essential elements are wanting which, in the eye of the law and political economy, give sanction to contract obligations. But we are constantly in the habit of assuming that this free choice and consent exist where there is really no choice or consent at all, and no intention of consenting; and the habit is fostered by the fictions to which lawyers, in their custom of referring all obligations to contract, are constantly resorting. We have no right to assume, as we constantly do, that, in matters which have become habitual, each person does or can exercise free choice whenever he makes what is termed a contract. Life would be intolerable if he did. Nine-tenths of the consequences of all our dealings are fixed for us by practice and by custom, and we are as unable to escape from these consequences as if they were enjoined by a specific statute. When we order a bale of goods, when we sell the produce of our land or our labour, when we take a railway ticket, when we send a packet by land or sea, when we insure our lives, our houses, our ships, or our goods,—in short, in almost every dealing of life, we subject ourselves to a series of conditions and consequences, many of which we do not and cannot know, and from many of which, did we know them, we should be absolutely incapable of freeing ourselves.

And yet, whenever a question arises in the law-courts as to the effect to be given to any of these conditions, the question which the lawyers put to themselves is almost always, "What did the parties mean?" and the conclusion at which they arrive is

C

justified or even sanctified in their eyes by the assumption of an implied promise, when, if the truth were told, in nine cases out of ten the parties had no meaning about it at all, having never contemplated the contingency which has arisen. And even if the question were put in the more plausible form, " What would they have intended if they had foreseen the contingency ?" it is still open to the observation that they might not, and in many cases would not, have been free agents in the matter. To say that a man must be held to have dealt with a view to all the consequences which law, which is the voice of the state, attaches to such dealings, may lead to the conclusions which justice and convenience require. But to say so leads us too often to ignore the fact that he did not as a matter of fact have these consequences in view, and that the state has really created them for him.

The case of the law of carriers and of innkeepers affords a good illustration. By the law of England the carrier was supposed to take the risk of loss or destruction of the goods committed to his care, and the innkeeper was held responsible for articles deposited by travellers in his inn. The lawyers added these stipulations to the actual contract, and justified the addition on the ground that it must have been what the parties intended. But as a matter of fact special stipulations to this effect were not made, and it is not likely that any carrier or innkeeper ever really intended to make such a stipulation. Indeed, so far were the added stipulations contrary to the real intentions of the parties that the state has been forced to step in afresh, and by special statute to modify and limit the liabilities which, by the action of the courts of law, it had itself created.

· It is quite possible that the conclusions of the law may be right, although arrived at by the fiction of an intention or a promise which never existed ; but the real absence of such an intention or promise shows how large a part the state plays, not only in enforcing what are ordinarily looked upon as the free and unfettered contracts of the parties, but in adding to them and in raising implications from them.

The state thus interferes with almost every mercantile dealing by adding to it a number of incidents which were not in the words, and often not in the minds, of the parties to the contract. This interference however forms part of the general mercantile law, and to attempt to describe its effect or to follow its application to particular mercantile contracts would carry us into a field far too wide for the scope of this treatise.

A further form of interference by the state of a similar kind is to be found in the numerous cases in which the legislature constantly interferes for the purpose of altering the existing legal incidents of a contract, leaving the parties either to adopt the altered law by allowing it to take its course, or to adopt other stipulations if they please. A well-known instance of this sort of interference is to be found in the recent Agricultural Holdings Act, which alters the existing consequences of a farming lease, and imposes new obligations on the landlord where there is no stipulation to the contrary. It is obvious that here there is no interference by the state with the freedom of the parties to contract, but simply with the custom or legal decisions which it has itself adopted as the

incidents of their contract when no other intention is
expressed.

We thus see that one most important function of the
state in relation to trade is to enforce contracts of
purchase and sale ; and to supply the deficiencies which
necessarily exist in all contracts by adding to them
those incidental consequences and conditions which, in
legal language, the parties must be supposed to have
contemplated, but which are, in fact, consequences and
conditions which the courts of law, having regard to
the ordinary practice of buyers and sellers, think to be
reasonable.   This function of the state is exercised by
courts of law, and almost escapes notice as a function of
the state from its universal application and the tacit
consent with which it is accepted.   We also see that it
is a further function of the state, acting through the
legislature, to see that these consequences and conditions
of a contract of sale are, from time to time, adapted to
the present wants of buyers and sellers ; to put an end
to such as are obsolete or injurious; and to add such
as the ever-varying and growing necessities of trade
require.

CHAPTER V.

It is, as stated in the last chapter, impossible in a work of this kind to do more than refer in the most general way to that great mass of rules by which the business of buying and selling is regulated, and to which we give the general name of Mercantile Law. This law is not . separated from the great body of our law by any definite line, for the remedies for non-payment of a debt or other non-performance of a contract are the same whether the cause of action has arisen out of buying or selling or out of any other relation. But there are certain large branches of law which, if not exclusively concerned with transactions of sale and exchange, are yet so intimately connected with those transactions that they may be said to owe their character and even their existence to them. A reference to some of these will show how wide and powerful is the influence which the state, regarded as the authoritative exponent of legal rules, plays in regulating all the doings of trade.

Debtor and Creditor.—The law of debtor and creditor constitutes a very large portion of our civil code. It is not exclusively mercantile, because, as noticed above, a debt may arise out of relations which have nothing to do with trade. But by far the greatest number of debts do arise directly or indirectly out of trading relations, and therefore of the whole law of debtor and creditor the greater part would have no existence but for trade.

Partnership is a relation which involves joint profit, and this profit is always made by some kind of trade. The law of partnership, therefore, with all its incidents, the rules which govern the creation and dissolution of partnerships, the relation of the partners to one another, and the rights and liabilities existing between them and third parties, are rules which the state adopts and enforces for the benefit of trade.

Joint-Stock Companies.—These are an extended form of partnership, requiring a special law of their own. This law fills one of the longest acts in the statute-book, and the act is supplemented by an ever-increasing mass of judicial decisions.

Principal and Agent.—This is a relation which, though it may exist independently of any commercial relation, does in the great proportion of cases arise out of such relations. In the present state of trade, when so many mercantile transactions are carried on between far distant places, and when the ever-growing magnitude of the business done and of the organisations by which it is done renders intermediate agency more and more extensive and more and more indispensable, the law of principal and agent is more than ever important to trade. The relations of principal and agent to one another and to third parties, embodied partly in statute law, but still more in judicial decisions, form a large and important branch of law.

Shipping.—This species of property is peculiar in many

respects, and has a special law of its own, which is to
be found in one of the longest acts in the statute-book,
in a great number of amending acts, and in innumerable
judicial decisions, besides constituting a considerable part
of that somewhat vague system of rules known as
international law.   On this subject more will be found
below in Chapter XIII.

Bills of Exchange.—This form of mercantile contract,
simple enough in its essential and original character, has
obtained such wide and varied use that it has given rise
to a complete system of special legal rules, which have
at last been codified in an act of the last session.[1]   The
case is interesting as an excellent illustration of the
way in which practice and custom grow into law; and
is therefore worthy of special notice.

A bill of exchange is, in its original form, an order
by a trader who is selling goods upon the trader to
whom they are sold to pay the price of them to some
third person.   The one trader may be in one place or
country, and the other in a different place or country.
When the order is acknowledged, or, in technical terms,
accepted, by the purchaser of the goods, the contract is
complete, and is performed by payment at the appointed
time.   This instrument, with the right to sue upon it,
is, unlike most other legal contracts, transferable by
mere delivery, and it is not necessary to prove that any
consideration has been paid for it.   Any person who in-
dorses it—*i.e.* places his name upon the back of it—
makes himself responsible for the payment to any subsequent holder.   Possessing these qualities, bills of
exchange become a valuable form of property.   They
are used for a great variety of purposes: they are a

---

[1] 45 & 46 Vict. ch. 61.

common form of credit, and to a large extent replace currency ; they are investments for bankers' deposits ; they constitute the ordinary means of remitting money from place to place, and of settling the balances of trade between different countries ; and the price paid for bills is an important index of the commercial and monetary relations existing between different nations. If it can be said with truth that modern trade could not go on without money, it may be said with equal truth that it could not go on without bills of exchange ; and the body of rules which govern them, though it has grown out of mercantile usage and not out of the direct action of government, is now no less the creature of the state than the law concerning the coinage.

Contracts with Carriers.—These again form a large and elaborate branch of the mercantile law, and are especially important in such a country as ours. They include contracts with railway companies for carrying and forwarding goods ; charter parties of ships ; and, above all, bills of lading for goods carried in ships, which are negotiable instruments, and carry with them by mere assignment the actual property in the goods which they represent.

Marine Insurance.—Policies of assurance, again, are contracts of the greatest importance to a mercantile country, and the difficult and complicated questions to which they have given rise between shipowners, owners of cargo, underwriters on ships, and underwriters on cargo, have called for decisions so numerous that they fill volumes of reports and text-books.

Formation of this Law.—The above are some of the principal branches of our law which owe their existence to, and which support and regulate, our trade, and it will

be seen from the above short reference to them how impossible it would be for trade to be carried on without
the action of the state which they involve.   It is true
that the greater part of this law has grown out of the
practice of traders, and is not due to the original or direct
action of the sovereign or the legislature.   Merchants
have done what they found useful, and the lawyers who
have been intrusted with the function of declaring the
law have very sensibly, by means of a useful fiction, declared the law to be what the merchants have practised,
wisely confining their own part in the matter to ascertaining the customs of trade and giving to those
customs form and logical consistency.   Finally, the
legislature has, in some cases, adopted the rules thus
determined, and has given them the form and sanction
of an Act of Parliament.   The case of bills of exchange
is an excellent illustration of the process of constructing
our mercantile law.   The assignment by delivery of a
right of action was a thing unknown to our earlier
common law; and the notion of a contract without consideration was abhorrent to the doctrines of courts of
equity.   But traders had found the convenience of the
modern bill of exchange which can be assigned by
delivery, and for which no consideration need be shown,
and wise judges adopted as law what the merchants had
adopted as practice.   An elaborate series of rules was
gradually worked out on this basis, and finally a code
containing these rules has been embodied in a printed
Act of Parliament.

It will however be found on consideration that in
every free and well-governed country, whether the
law has had its apparent origin in a decree of a sovereign, or in an act of a representative legislature, or

in the adoption by judges of an existing practice as law, the law thus adopted and declared is really an expression of a popular want, and a sanction given in the name of the collective nation to a rule which it needs and of which it approves. Our Mercantile Law is, fortunately, more than any other branch of law the direct outcome of the needs and practices of trade, and to this it owes its great excellence. But it is not the less on this account the voice of the state.

Operation of this Law.—When it is said that the law regulates all mercantile transactions, it must not be supposed that its active operation is consciously and generally felt. The law acts as a guide and a scarecrow, but it is seldom necessary to apply for its compulsory intervention. Take the law of debtor and creditor : every debt can be enforced at law ; but out of the many millions of debts which are incurred every day, the number which are enforced at law is small indeed. We often hear of commercial dishonesty, but it is the exception, and a rare exception. The more surprising thing is to think of the innumerable transactions which are completed, the millions of money which change hands daily, on the faith of a word or a scrap of paper, without even the consciousness of a legal obligation. Honesty is not only the best policy, it is the one essential virtue of a trading community. Law is appealed to only in very exceptional cases of distinct roguery, or in cases where real doubt exists as to what the obligation ought to be. The law is not felt at all in the great majority of cases where its intervention is not required. Hence the value of civil liability as a remedy for wrong, as compared with the favourite remedy of direct administrative supervision. Where it can be made the duty

of men to perform a given duty or to abstain from a
given injurious practice, where this duty can be made
the foundation for a civil suit at law, and where
it is sufficiently to the interest of their fellow-men
to make them abstain, an action for damages by the
person injured is not only the most efficient remedy,
but it has the great advantage that it is applied only
in the particular cases in which a remedy is needed,
and does not, like the supervision of an executive
officer, interfere with all the innocent operations of
ordinary dealings.

CHAPTER VI

GENERAL LIMITATIONS BY THE STATE OF CONTRACT OBLIGATIONS.

It is, as we have seen, a most important function of the state to enforce the obligations of trading contracts, and in so doing to add largely to those obligations. It also interferes by imposing a great number of limitations on these obligations. Of these limitations some are general in character, restricting under certain circumstances the power or right to enter into any such obligations, and restricting or abolishing under certain circumstances the binding power of such obligations. These general limitations form the subject of the present chapter.

Personal Disabilities.—An infant, a drunken man, and a lunatic cannot trade at all; they are not allowed to bind themselves by any contract obligation to a person who knows their condition.

A married woman's power of trading has hitherto been limited; but this limitation is done away with by a statute of the last session (45 & 46 Vict. ch. 75), which gives her complete control over her own property, enables her to bind herself and it by trading contracts, and makes her subject to the bankruptcy law.

A trader cannot bind himself by any general contract. not to exercise a lawful trade, and contracts for a strike or lock-out cannot therefore be enforced at law.

An alien enemy, *i.e.* the subject of a state with which we are at war, cannot trade with us; but an alien friend can do everything in the way of trade which a British subject can do, with the exception that he cannot own British ships.

Certain traders are required to obtain licenses before exercising their trades. They are—apothecaries, auctioneers, brewers, brokers, chimney-sweepers, distillers, game dealers, goldsmiths, marine-store dealers, patent medicine sellers, pawnbrokers, playing-card makers, pedlars, publicans, tobacco sellers, and vinegar makers. In some of these cases the object is the public health; in some, the protection of the public revenue; in one, humanity; whilst in some cases the reason for requiring a license is not obvious.

Limited Liability.—In this place we may notice an important disability which the state, acting through the law-courts, formerly imposed on a certain form of trading, but which is now removed; a disability which, whilst it existed, prevented, or at any rate checked and obstructed, one of the most important factors in modern industry—joint-stock enterprise.

When joint-stock undertakings were first established, the courts of law insisted on applying to them the doctrines and rules of procedure of the old law of partnership, which, besides being cumbrous and utterly inapplicable, made it essential that every shareholder should be liable to the whole extent of his fortune for all the debts of the concern.   This doctrine was modified in the case of parliamentary companies by private Acts of Parliament, and in some other cases by Royal Charter.   But it was not till the passing of a bill introduced by Mr. Lowe in 1856 that full power was given to joint-stock associations to incorporate themselves with a proper organisation, and with limited liability.   The act was extended to banks in 1858, and the whole law was amended and consolidated in 1862. Since the passing of these acts, all persons have been able to organise themselves for any lawful purpose, and to undertake commercial dealings with others on the terms of either limited or unlimited liability on the part of their members.   From a parliamentary return in 1877 it appears that the paid-up capital of companies registered under the Joint-Stock Companies Act exceeded £300,000,000.   This is of course exclusive of parliamentary companies, such as railway companies, and also of companies formed under charters.

There is probably no feature in modern society which has effected so great a revolution in trade and industry as joint-stock enterprise ; and this enterprise could scarcely have existed under the fetters which the state formerly imposed upon it.   The case is extremely interesting as an illustration of the important part which the state may play in checking or developing industry, and also of the mischief it may do, almost without notice, by an impolitic restriction.

Statute of Frauds, 29 Car. II. ch. 3.—By this statute any ' contract for the sale of goods for more than £10 is void unless it is in writing and signed by the parties or their agents, or unless there has been delivery and acceptance of the goods or of part of them, or payment or part payment by the buyer. The litigation on this section has been very great. One judge is reported to have said that every word of the section was worth a king's ransom, and a second judge to have retorted that every word had cost a king's ransom. I believe that until quite recently every contract for the purchase and sale of cotton sold at Liverpool was rendered invalid at law under this enactment, and that a very large part of these contracts are still invalid. So difficult is it for the state to interfere judiciously with mercantile dealings; and so ineffectual is the interference of the state when it runs counter to the practice which buyers and sellers, for their own convenience, adopt.

Statute of Limitations, 21 James I. ch. 16.—In the absence of special stipulation to the contrary, an unexecuted contract would never be at an end; the obligation would remain hanging over the heads of the parties for ever. It has therefore been the policy of every civilised government to fix a period beyond which it will give no assistance to enforce contracts. In the case of contracts for the purchase and sale of goods, this period was fixed by the statute of 21 James I. ch. 16, at six years, and this period of limitation still remains. It is generally put by the lawyers on the ground of the legal maxim, *Interest reipublicæ ut sit finis litium;* but the more intelligible ground is that it is not right that a man should remain for an indefinite time the slave of an obligation which there has been no attempt to enforce.

At the present time, when there is a constantly growing tendency to curtail credit, when the steamship, the railway, and the telegraph, have accelerated mercantile operations, and when the period for which bills have to run is becoming shorter and shorter ; when a number of wholesale transactions are completed at once for cash ; when of retail transactions many, if not most, are for ready money ; when many tradesmen's bills are paid weekly, and few run for as long as a year—the period of six years is much longer than is necessary. For most of the transactions of daily life one year would be ample, and if the effect of shortening the period were in some instances to prevent credit from being given, and in others to make the seller insist on earlier payment, the effect would be a very wholesome one. Here, again, it is important to remember that the real interference of the state with freedom is where it enforces contracts ; and that, when it refuses to insist on their being performed, by that refusal it restores freedom.

Bankruptcy.—(The Bankruptcy Act, 1869, 32 & 33 Vict. ch. 71, and Debtors Act, 1869, 32 & 33 Vict. ch. 62, contain the present law on this subject.) Bankruptcy, again, is a case in which the state refuses, under certain circumstances, to follow the usual rule of enforcing individual contracts, and substitutes a special mode of proceeding, the ultimate effect of which is generally to free the contracting party from the obligations which he has taken upon himself. It is so far like the Statute of Limitations that it is a restoration of freedom, although upon certain stringent conditions. The general features of the bankruptcy law are as follows :—

When a man has incurred a number of debts and is unable to pay them, he may be made a bankrupt. The consequence is that all the property which then belongs to him becomes divisible amongst his creditors, and that if the court gives him a certificate of discharge—

which it does unless a special case of misconduct is made
out against him—he is discharged from his obligations,
and left free to acquire and enjoy property and to begin
the world again. Special provision is made for punishing
fraudulent debtors, and, in cases where a debtor can
pay, but refuses to pay, there is still vested in the court
a power of imprisonment. But for mere debt with
inability to pay no man can be imprisoned. On these
general principles there is now no dispute, and they are
admitted as the foundation of every bankruptcy bill.
Nor is there now any real distinction of importance
between traders and other persons, or between bankruptcy and insolvency : it is admitted that all debtors,
whether in what is called trade or not, must be subject
to the same law of debtor and creditor.

There has thus been a great advance since the time
when men charged with non-payment of debts were
imprisoned both on mesne process, *i.e.*, before any
judicial sentence, and also after judgment ; when our
gaols were full of debtors ; and when, unless a man was
what the law recognised as a trader, he could not, even
when discharged from prison, earn or acquire property
freed from his previous debts. We ought not to forget
this when we hear so many complaints against the
present law of bankruptcy. It is not likely that that
law will ever give entire satisfaction. Where a creditor
gets only half a crown or five shillings in the pound out
of what is due to him, he is not likely to think the
proceeding by which he gets it a satisfactory one ; nor
is it likely that any process of liquidation can be established which will not waste much of the assets in
expenses. But the establishment of the principles—
that when a man is unable to pay his debts, his

D

property should be divided among his creditors; that mere inability to pay should not carry with it penal consequences; that an innocent debtor should be free to trade and acquire property again; and that misconduct in incurring debt should be distinguished from mere insolvency, and should be punished accordingly —shows that, whatever imperfections there still are in the law of bankruptcy, real progress has been made towards placing that law on a satisfactory footing.

There are however points of great importance in which our bankruptcy law is still confessedly and mischievously defective. These relate principally to the collection and distribution of assets, and to the exposure and punishment of culpable debtors.

An attempt was made in 1832 to collect and distribute the assets of the bankrupt by official agency, under the control of the court. This agency was at first successful, but ultimately broke down, probably in consequence of the want of that administrative supervision which a court of law is not fitted to give. The collection and distribution of assets was in 1869 handed over to the creditors, without official, and even, in most cases, without judicial control; and the consequence is found to be that, as it is not worth the while of the creditors generally to spend time or trouble in looking after bad debts, the management of the business falls into the hands of a class of agents whose only object is to make as much as they can for themselves out of it.

Again, in placing the collection of assets in the hands of the creditors, no provision was made for enforcing that part of the law which provided for the exposure and punishment of fraudulent or otherwise culpable dealings. Gross frauds and misconduct consequently

escape censure and punishment, and are not even
brought to the notice of the court of bankruptcy, which,
like other courts of law, can only act upon charges and
evidence brought before it.

To remedy these evils it has been proposed in recent
attempts at bankruptcy legislation, to allow no debtor
to obtain the benefits of bankruptcy without public
inquiry and examination ; to give to the creditors the
assistance of an official agency, responsible to a minister
of the Crown, which shall aid, but not control them,
in managing, collecting, holding, and distributing the
assets ; and to intrust to the same official agency the
duty of inquiring whether the debtor has been guilty of
criminal misconduct, and, if he has, of bringing it
before the bankruptcy court with a view to the refusal
or suspension of his discharge or before the public
prosecutor, with a view to criminal proceedings. The
inquiry would be analogous in character to a coroners'
inquest, or to the more modern inquiries which now
take place into shipwrecks, and into railway and mining
accidents. If it is the duty of the state to inquire into
the causes of accidents which cause injury to life
and limb, it is at least equally necessary in a mercantile
country like ours to make inquiry into collapses of
credit which affect our national character, and often
bring want and misery into a thousand homes.

A further point of great interest in any new bankruptcy scheme is the question of making some proceeding
analogous to bankruptcy applicable to the case of
workmen who have little or nothing but their weekly
wages, so that they may, in case of insolvency, be able
at moderate cost and on reasonable terms, to obtain
their discharge, and so that the sentences of imprison-

ment which county court judges now inflict for wilful non-payment of small debts, may be reduced within the smallest possible compass.

Bills of Sale.—These are in form instruments by which goods and chattels are sold; but as goods and chattels are generally transferred and pass by delivery, bills of sale are little needed for the purpose of actual sale, and are generally used as securities for the advance of money, the possession of the goods remaining with the original owner, and the grantee having the right in default of payment of interest or principal, to seize, sell, and realise.   Under these circumstances the legislature, in order to give notice of the real state of the owner-ship, has long required bills of sale to be registered; and by a recent act, which purported to surround them with additional precautions, bills of sale when duly registered were made to take the property out of the operation of those clauses of the Bankruptcy Act which provide that goods left by the true owner in the possession and apparent order and disposition of the bankrupt, shall be treated as forming part of the debtor's assets for the benefit of general creditors.   The effect of this, coupled with other circumstances, appears to have been very unfortunate.   Bills of sale have multiplied enormously; the precautions which it was supposed would secure needy persons against granting improvi-dent bills of sale, have operated in the contrary direction; poor artisans have been victimised by money-lenders; and wholesale dealers and other creditors have found that the goods on which they relied as belonging to their debtor, and which in many cases they supplied themselves on credit, were seized and carried off under the powers of a bill of sale, the existence of which they did

not suspect.   So difficult is it to interfere successfully,
or foresee the consequences of interference.

Under these circumstances the legislature, by an Act
45 & 46 Vict. ch. 43, passed in the session of 1882, after
full discussion before select committees of both Houses,
has, besides restoring the operation of the "order and
disposition" clauses of the Bankruptcy Act, provided
that no bill of sale is to convey after-acquired goods;
and that no bill of sale is to be given for any sum less
than £30.   It will be interesting to see whether these
provisions prove to be effectual in protecting helpless
persons, and in preventing fraudulent transactions;
whether they will be found to be open to evasion; and
whether they will hamper legitimate transactions.

CHAPTER VII.

A FURTHER function of the state is to settle the terms
in which trading transactions are carried on. It does
this in two ways. First, it prescribes certain measures
of weight and size in which the quantities of articles
sold are to be described, and it gives the means of
ascertaining that these measures are accurate. Secondly,
it both determines, and stamps and issues, the money
in which the value of all goods bought and sold is
measured, and by means which, as a medium, they are
exchanged. The utility of this function is obvious.
In the simplest and rudest form of trading, one article
would be exchanged against another, without any
description or definition except such as would arise
out of the direct impression made by the particular
articles on the senses of the two parties. An apron-
ful of corn would be exchanged against an armful
of meat, or against a hewn tree or stone; but there
would be nothing by which the quantities of any of
these articles could be known, or by which, in the

absence of the articles themselves, any of the parties could tell what he was giving or getting. Nor would there be any common measure of value to which each could be referred. The person possessing the corn, and wanting meat, wood, or stone, must wait until he could find a person possessing the requisite piece of meat, or of wood, or stone, and at the same time wanting corn, and then the two parties must come together and compare their respective articles by the use of their unassisted senses.

Contrast this with the sale by the butcher of so many pounds of beef at so many pence a pound ; the purchase by the miller of so many bushels of wheat at so many shillings a bushel ; or by the builder of so many feet of timber at so many pence a foot. The facilities of dealing in the latter case as compared with the former are obvious. But these facilities would be impossible if we did not know accurately and universally what was meant by a pound, and by a foot, and by a bushel, and by a shilling, and by a penny : and in order that they may be accurately and universally known, they must be determined in such a way that all persons must accept them, and this can only be done by the authority of the state. It has therefore been admitted in all civilised societies that the state must determine measures of weight, size, and value.

The following passages are an excellent illustration of the way in which barter of actual commodities becomes a commercial exchange with a common measure of value. They are extracted from a chapter in Butler's *Great Lone Land*, giving a vivid picture of the scene at one of the Hudson's Bay Companies settlements when the Red Indians come to exchange their skins and furs and pemmican, for blankets and beads, guns, and ammunition. He says (p. 283) :—

"Money values are entirely unknown in these trades. The values of articles are computed by 'skins'; for instance, a horse will be reckoned at sixty skins, and these sixty skins will be given thus : a gun, fifteen skins; a capote, ten skins ; a blanket, ten skins; ball and powder, ten skins ; tobacco, fifteen skins, total sixty skins. The Bull Ermine, or the Four Bears, or the Red Daybreak, or whatever may be the brave's name, hands over the horse and gets in return a blanket, a gun, a capote, ball and powder, and tobacco. The term 'skin' is a very old one in the fur trade ; the original standard, the beaver skin—or as it was called 'the made beaver'—was the medium of exchange, and every other skin and article of trade was graduated upon the scale of the beaver; thus a beaver or a skin was reckoned equivalent to one mink skin, one marten was equal to two skins, one black fox twenty skins, and so on in the same manner, a blanket, a capote, a gun, or a kettle, had their different values in skins."

Then, after describing the scene in which the dealing takes place, he goes on :—

"Sometimes when the stock of pemmican or robes is small, the braves object to see their 'pile' go for a little parcel of tea or sugar. The steelyard and weighing balance are their especial objects of dislike. 'What for you put on one side tea or sugar, and on the other a little bit of iron?' they say; 'we don't know what that medicine is. But look here, put on one side of that thing that swings a bag of pemmican, and put on the other side blankets and tea and sugar, and then when the two sides stop swinging, you take the bag of pemmican and we will take the blankets and the tea ; that would be fair, for one side will be as big as the other.' This is a very bright idea on the part of the

Four Bears, and elicits universal satisfaction all round.
Four Bears and his brethren are however a little bit
put out of conceit when the trader observes, 'Well,
let it be as you say. We will make the balance swing
level between the bag of pemmican and the blankets;
but we will carry out the idea still further. You will
put your marten skins, and your otter and fisher skins
on one side; I will put against them on the other my
blankets and my gun and ball and powder, then when
both sides are level you will take the ball and powder
and the blankets, and I will take the marten and the
rest of the fine furs.' This proposition throws a new
light upon the question of weighing machines and
steelyards, and after some little deliberation it is
resolved to abide by the old plan of letting the white
trader decide the weight himself in his own way, for
it is clear that the steelyard is a great medicine which
no brave can understand, and which can only be
manipulated by a white medicine-man."

Weights and Measures.—These are now determined
under the authority of the Weights and Measures Act
(1878, 41 and 42 Vict. chap. 49). In France, when
they adopted their convenient decimal system, they
endeavoured to found their ultimate standard on a
natural and unconventional basis by taking as their
metre a fraction of the circumference of the earth,
and they deduced all other weights and measures
from it, using a decimal system of division and multiplication. But as a matter of fact any such natural
basis is impracticable; all ultimate standards must
be arbitrary; and the French metre is only a particular piece of metal duly marked, which is kept in
Paris. The ultimate English standards consist of a
bronze bar on which a yard is marked, and of a
platinum pound weight, kept in the Standards depart-

ment of the Board of Trade. These are called the imperial standards. From this yard and pound four exact copies have been made, of which one is kept at the Mint, one at the Royal Society, one at the Observatory at Greenwich, and one is immured in the wall of the Houses of Parliament. These are called the parliamentary standards. Other copies of the yard and pound have been made from these, and are kept as practical standards for daily use at the Board of Trade. From these two original measures, the yard and the pound, all other legal weights and measures, whether they denote weight, length, area, or capacity, are derived by combination, multiplication and division. Standards of all such physical weights and measures as are used in trade are made and kept at the Board of Trade, and new ones are added from time to time as the wants of trade alter. They are kept in an office in Palace Yard which was formerly part of the Old Palace at Westminster, and which is not inappropriately devoted to what has from time immemorial been a royal function.

From these Board of Trade standards of ordinary weights and measures, further copies are made for local use by the authorities of towns and counties, and these local standards are from time to time verified by comparison with the Board of Trade standards. Inspectors are appointed by the local authorities for their respective districts, and it is their business to see that the weights and measures used in trade are truthful and accurate, and for this purpose to compare them with the local standards.

Every dealing in any article which is sold by weight or measure must be made in one of the legalised standards. Every publication of the prices of any such articles must be in the like terms, and no weight or measure is allowed to be kept for use in trade which does not correspond in denomination with one of the legalised Board of Trade standards.

I have said above that the universal knowledge and use of weights and measures within the country is an essential condition of their value, and a reason for giving to the state the power of determining them. Under the present circumstances of international trade this is not sufficient, and a demand is arising for an international system of weights and measures. Most countries in Europe are adopting the French metric system. In this country the only step we have taken in this direction is to allow persons to make use of the terms of the metric system in making contracts. But we do not allow any physical metric weights and measures to be kept for use in trade. A merchant may contract to sell cloth or cotton by the metre instead of by the yard; but he may not keep a metre in his shop or warehouse by which to measure it. This is absurd and illogical enough. But so long as we retain our own system, with the great variety of actual weights and measures founded on the pound and yard which the necessities of trade require, it would probably lead to great confusion and even to fraud, were we to add to the multitude of actual legal weights and measures now in use the further number which would be necessary in order to give practical effect to the metric system. So long as our system differs from that of our neighbours we are in a dilemma. Upon the difficulty of changing our system it is unnecessary to dilate.

Gold and Silver Money.—But the state not only

determines the terms in which the size and weight of articles sold shall be described, it also stamps and issues money, and in so doing both determines the terms in which their value must be stated, which, when so stated, we know as price; and supplies, though not at its own cost, the medium by means of which they are bought and sold.

The following is the definition of money given in Lord Liverpool's *Coins of the Realm*, and of the metals of which it is made :

"The money or coin of a country is the standard measure by which the value of all things bought and sold is regulated and ascertained, and it is itself, at the same time, the value, or equivalent, for which goods are exchanged, and in which contracts are generally made payable. In this last respect, money, as a measure, differs from all others, and to the combination of the two qualities before defined, which constitute the essence of money, the principal difficulties that attend it in speculation and practice, both as a measure and an equivalent, are to be ascribed. These two qualities can never be brought perfectly to unite and agree; for if money were a measure alone, and made, like all other measures, of a material of little or no value, it would not answer the purpose of an equivalent. And if it is made in order to answer the purpose of an equivalent, of a material of value, subject to frequent variations, according to the price at which such material sells at the market, it fails on that account in the quality of a standard or measure, and will not continue to be perfectly uniform and at all times the same. Civilised nations have generally adopted gold and silver as the material of their money because these metals are costly and difficult to procure, little subject to variation in value, durable, divisible, and easily stamped or marked."

Of the coins used in our currency the pound is the real standard of value, and gold sovereigns are the only coin which is legal tender for debts exceeding forty shillings. The gold sovereign consists of a certain fixed fraction of an ounce of pure gold with a certain quantity of alloy. The essential function of the Mint consists in seeing that its weight and purity are what the law requires, and in stamping and issuing it so that it may be known everywhere as certified by the Government to possess these qualities. Beyond this the Government does nothing to determine its value, which is simply the value of that quantity of gold in the open market. We often hear the *Mint price* of gold spoken of, which is fixed by law at £3 17s. 10½d. an ounce, and this is apt to be confusing, since what we call "prices" generally vary with supply and demand. But by the *Mint price* of gold is only meant the quantity of sovereigns and fractions of a sovereign into which the Mint divides the gold which is brought to it for coinage; and it is important to remember that by the shillings and pence which form part of the *Mint price* are meant, not given quantities of silver or bronze, but the fractions of a gold sovereign which are known by these names. The *Mint price* of an ounce of gold thus means simply that an ounce in weight of gold is divided into three whole sovereigns and $\frac{17}{20}$ ths, and $\frac{10}{240}$ ths, and $\frac{1}{480}$ th of a gold sovereign.

But we could not be sure that the gold sovereign would be of the value of the gold contained in it if the Government had the power to increase or diminish the quantity of sovereigns coined at their own discretion, and thus to determine what quantity of currency the people shall use. It is therefore made incumbent on the Mint to coin all the gold which is brought to it for coinage, or which comes to the same thing, to give for all the gold which is brought to it an equivalent quantity of gold coins. The quantity of coins in circulation must therefore depend entirely on the demand for them, and not on the action of the Government. If more coins are needed, gold is brought to the Mint and turned into coins. If fewer coins are needed, existing sovereigns are melted down and exported or otherwise used. The value of the coin must therefore be that of the gold used in making it, with nothing added but the value of the Government certificate of its weight and purity. It is this self-acting character of the Mint which is the great safeguard of the coinage. If it were in the power of the Government to refuse to coin, they would be able to restrict the coinage, and to add to its exchangeable value. If they were able to alter the quantity and purity of the metal contained in the sovereign, they would be able to depreciate its value, as has in former times often been done. In either case they would be able to derange markets and alter existing contracts which are made in terms of the pound. The self-acting character of the Mint operations reduces the function of the state in issuing money to that of a verifier of weights and measures.

With regard to the silver coinage the case is different. It is not a legal tender for more than 40s.; the value of the coin measured in gold is rather more than the value of the metal it contains. The Mint price of silver is 5s. 6d. an ounce, in other words, for an ounce of pure silver the Mint gives 66d.; but the price of silver in the market is now about 52d. an ounce, so that the value of the shilling is considerably more than the market value of the silver of which it consists.

The silver coins are not therefore a standard of value at all; they are a token coinage, only used for small transactions; and when a silver coin is spoken of as denoting the price of any article, what is meant by it is the fraction of the gold sovereign to which it corresponds. If we say that mutton is worth a shilling a pound, we mean that a pound of mutton is worth one-twentieth of a gold sovereign; if we say that wheat is 50s. a quarter, we mean that a quarter of wheat is worth two gold sovereigns and a half. Under this system the action of the Government in respect of silver coins differs from its action in respect to gold coins. In the case of gold coins, the Mint is obliged to coin all the gold which is brought to it, or, which comes to the same thing, to give gold coins for it—in short, to turn all the gold brought to it into gold coins. In the case of silver it is not under any such obligation, but it is bound to make and give silver coin when demanded in return for gold coin, to give twenty shillings in silver for every gold sovereign presented to it.

The supply of silver coins needed for the retail dealings of the country is easily effected through the banks. When they find that their customers want silver, they demand it through the Bank of England from the Mint, and pay for it in gold coins. They have no motive to ask for more than is really wanted by the country as silver currency; for the silver in the coins would be worth less if melted down for use in the arts or for exportation than it is worth as silver coin. The Mint buy the silver needed to make the required coin and make a profit by the difference between the market value of the silver and the price in gold given for it. But as they only issue it in accordance with the demands made for it by the bankers, they have no power to flood the market with silver coins or to depreciate its value. Their function is therefore really automatic in respect of silver as well as gold, and their real business is to verify the quality and quantity of the silver and to make and stamp the coins accordingly.

In order that the Mint may perform its function of verifying the quality of the gold and silver used in coinage, there must be a standard of quality. This is found in certain plates of gold and silver—called the pyx—which are kept with other standards by the Board of Trade, and which are produced annually on the trial of the pyx, when a jury of the Goldsmiths' Company compare samples of the metal used by the Mint in coinage with the standard plates. These standard plates were formerly kept in a chapel opening into the cloisters of Westminster Abbey, called the Chapel of the Pyx, in which the king's treasures used to be stored, and on the door of which is still to be seen a trace of the skin of a malefactor flayed alive for trying to rob the king's treasury. The Board of Trade wished to hand this chapel over to the Dean and Chapter, within whose precincts it lies, but the late Dean Stanley characteristically refused to receive it on the ground that the retention of this interesting spot in the precincts of the Abbey by a department of the state which has to do with the regulation of trade was a symbolic link in the relations of the state to the Church.

What is true of silver is also generally true of the copper, or rather, the bronze, coinage. The metal employed in the bronze coin is worth less than the fraction of the gold sovereign which it is used to express, and it is not a legal tender for more than 12*d*. The Mint issues it from time to time in different districts, and contracts the issue when it is found to be superabundant.

It will therefore be seen that gold is the sole ultimate measure of value in this country, and that its value as compared with other commodities is determined precisely in the same way as that of other commodities, viz., by supply and demand; in other words, it is the value which people will give for it. The sole function of the Government is to ascertain the quality and weight of the gold, and to give it a stamp denoting that quality and weight. Other coins are measured in gold, and do not pass according to their own intrinsic or market value; they are tokens, not articles of commerce. The function of the Government with respect to them is to supply any number for which the corresponding price in gold is given; to verify the quantity and quality of the metal they contain; and to stamp them accordingly.

Bimetallism. — As the question of bimetallism has been much discussed of late, it may be well to mention what is the meaning of it. It is obvious that the selection of gold as the standard of value is arbitrary. Most nations have selected either gold or silver as their standard of value, and as the material for their principal coins, because, as above noticed, these metals are scarce, and therefore possess a high value; are easily divisible; are readily stamped and marked; and are comparatively indestructible. Some nations have preferred gold; some have preferred silver: some have taken both. England, after many years' trial of both,

E

has now for a century and more adopted gold as the sole standard of value; and it has done so because it was found, that when both gold and silver were standards of value and when both could be coined to an unlimited extent, people preferred to pay their debts in the metal which was for the time the cheaper, and the dearer metal was exported. At that time there was no arrangement between nations for a common system of coinage or common measure of value nor was any such arrangement thought of as possible.

The bimetallists say that such a system is now possible, and that many nations, especially those which have silver as a standard of value, would be only too glad to join England in a system which would fix the relative values of gold and silver, and make both metals equally the standard of value and the materials of coinage. They appear to argue that the value of the precious metals depends on the demand for them; that the principal demand for them is for purposes of currency; and that governments can therefore, in adopting them as currency, do for them what they cannot do for other articles, viz.—create and regulate the demand and fix their relative value. The advantages they propose from bimetallism are as follows :— First, that if we could have the two precious metals as standards of value instead of one, the fluctuations of each would be neutralised, and the standard of value would be on the whole steadier than it is now. Secondly, that the scarcity and consequent rise in the value of gold, which under present circumstances there is too much reason to apprehend, would be prevented if silver could be brought to the aid of gold. Thirdly, that the trade between gold-using countries and silver-using coun.

tries would be made much easier if they had a common standard of value, and if the fluctuations of value between silver and gold could be eliminated. The monometallists, on the other hand, urge the following arguments :—First, that the suggested arrangement between the nations is probably impracticable, and if made, could not be relied on. Secondly, that if such an arrangement could be made, it would at this time be suicidal in England, which possesses an immense store of gold, and to which large debts in gold are now owing. to depreciate the value of her property and claims by a measure which must raise the present low value of silver as compared with gold. Thirdly, and principally, that it would be impossible by any artificial law, municipal or international, to tie together gold and silver so that the value of the one measured by the other should never fluctuate. The great merit of our present monometallic system of coinage, they say, is, that it is automatic ; that there is in it nothing arbitrary, nothing which depends on the action of governments ; that the value of gold is a matter of supply and demand, and that upon this value the whole system is based, whereas under the bimetallic system an attempt is made to fix an arbitrary relation between the values of two metals which have no natural dependence on or connection with each other. Value, they say further, depends on the two factors of demand and supply, and admitting that governments may, in adopting one or both of the metals as currency, have some control over the demand, the control they thus possess is very incomplete and imperfect, whilst they have no control at all over the supply. The monometallists urge in addition that the apprehended dangers of the monometallic system and advantages of the bimetallic system are chimerical or exaggerated; that a rise in the value of gold, if it takes place, or a fall in the value of silver, will cause no such change or inconvenience as is apprehended; and that the inconveniences to trade arising from the use of two different metals and from fluctuations in their value, are as nothing compared with the inconveniences arising from other causes of fluctuation, such as the use of paper money, or the constantly recurring changes in the supply and demand of articles of commerce, inconveniences, to which trade must always be subject, and in spite of which it flourishes. Under these circumstances, say the monometallists, it would be madness to change a system which has worked well, and is in accordance with the theory on which our coinage is based; and as they have in addition to their arguments, the advantage of possession, it is not likely at present, at any rate, that the advocates of bimetallism will make much way in this country.

Paper Money.—A written or printed promise to pay, issued by a banker and payable on demand, will, if people trust the banker, perform many of the functions of money. It is circulated like the coins which it promises, and is received in payment of debts. Such paper money, as it is called, has been the subject of endless controversy. Whether it should be issued by any one except the state or the agents of the state; what should be the lowest sum for which it should be given; whether it should in any case be inconvertible, *i.e.*, whether any such paper should be allowed to circulate for which the holder has not the right at any moment to claim payment in coin; and whether convertibility is a sufficient security against depreciation, and also against excessive issue, are questions, some of which are still unsettled. But all reasonable people are satisfied that no such paper money ought to be inconvertible. To substitute for hard coin paper promises to pay, is a mode of raising money to which nations in difficulties are not unfrequently driven. But, like all other attempts to make something out of nothing by operation of law, such a step is sure to cause loss, confusion, and inconvenience; and all nations retrace it, often at considerable loss, as soon as they can afford to do so. It is also, I think, generally admitted, at least in England, that the issue of paper money, especially if it is made a legal tender for the payment of debts, is a proper function of the state, and that if any profit is made by the issue it is a profit which should belong to the state.

In England the issue of notes by bankers was long since limited, in order to preserve the monopoly of the Bank of England, and since 1821, the lowest sum for which notes can be issued, whether by the Bank of England or others, has been limited to £5. This limitation does not however extend to Scotland or Ireland. The bank note circulation is now governed by Sir R. Peel's celebrated Act of 1844, 7 & 8 Vict. chap. 32.[1] The principle on which these Acts were founded is that paper money should only be issued by the state or the agents of the state; that paper money should not only be convertible, but that it should vary in quantity in the same manner and proportions as the metal which it represents; and that for this purpose paper money should only be issued against actual bullion lying in the

[1] For the Scotch and Irish Acts, see 8 and 9 Vict. chaps. 37, 38.

hands of the issuer. Out of regard for existing facts
and interests this theory was not strictly applied.
Existing private bankers were allowed to continue their
previous amount of issues, but their notes are not legal
tender. The banking department and the issue department of the Bank of England were separated. The
Bank of England, in consideration of a debt due from
the Government to the Bank, were authorised to issue
notes to the extent of £14,000,000, since somewhat
increased. This amount was taken as an amount below
which the paper in circulation, had never, even in times
of panic, been known to be reduced. Beyond this the
Bank must, for every note they issue, have gold or silver
bullion in their coffers. They are bound to give notes
for all gold brought to them, paying for it £3 17s. 9d.
an ounce, instead of the Mint price of £3 17s. 10½d., so
as to renumerate them for the expense of the issue ;
and they are bound to pay their notes in full whenever
presented. Their notes are legal tender everywhere
except at their own counters.

The effect of this limitation of the paper currency on
commercial dealings has been the subject of endless
controversy, and the Act has three times been suspended,
once in the crisis of 1847, once in that of 1857, and
once again in 1866. On all three occasions the issue
department of the Bank placed at the disposal of the
banking department £2,000,000 of notes against the
same sum in consols, though on two occasions the banking department did not find it necessary actually to use
any of the excessive issue. On all those occasions the
suspension was successful in allaying panic. What has
happened before will no doubt happen again. If a
commercial panic should recur in which people are

willing to trust Bank of England notes when they will trust no other form of credit, Bank of England notes will be created to meet the emergency, even if they operate only as a cordial, and not as solid food.

But the controversy on the principles of the Act of 1844 has now slackened. Most economists, I believe, now think that whatever importance is to be attached to bank notes, and to their effect on prices and speculation, and whether the principle of the Act of 1844 is sound or not, and whether the whole operation is beneficial or not, the most effectual way of maintaining a proper reserve of coin, and of checking an efflux of gold which might lead to insecurity and panic, is to be found in raising the rate of interest for loans of money in due time, and in keeping that rate at a proper amount. How far the Bank of England, which at one time was able to control the rate of interest, and whose action is still looked upon as indicating what the rate of interest actually is, or is likely to be, or ought to be, will, in the face of its numerous competitors, be able to perform this useful function satisfactorily; and, if it proves to be unable to do so, what organisation should be substituted, are questions of much interest. They are not entirely foreign to the subject of this treatise, but are too speculative and too difficult to be discussed here.

Demand for Currency.—This chapter is not complete without pointing out the effect of growing population and business on the demand for currency. On the one hand the enormous increase of purchases and of hired services tends to raise the demand for, and consequently to increase the value of, gold and silver. On the other hand, the ingenuity of modern trade is constantly devising new substitutes for cash. Transfers of book credits; bills of exchange; cheques; telegraphic transfers; transfers of stocks and securities; all the various expedients for which our banking system affords facilities; render the use of cash almost unnecessary except in small and retail transactions, and thus check the increased demand for gold and silver coin which would otherwise materially derange our standards of value.

CHAPTER VIII.

I HAVE shown that the state takes a part in every trade transaction by compelling the parties to it to perform their bargains; that it interferes farther to limit this compulsion and to put an end to the bargains in certain cases; that it also prescribes the terms in which they shall be made. But having done this, the broad principle acted on in this country is that the state should leave the parties to themselves. It does not confine the sale of any article to any particular person, nor does it attempt to fix prices. On the contrary, it carefully avoids any attempt to create monopolies, and regards prices and values as matters which can only be regulated by demand and supply.

This was not always so, nor is it so now in all foreign civilised countries. In former times there was an assize which fixed the price of bread and ale in England. The price of bread is or can still be fixed by law in France: and in many countries the governments still possess the monopoly of certain articles, such as salt, tobacco, and opium.

In former times the government of this country also

claimed and exercised the right of restricting buying and selling, by granting to particular persons monopolies of the sale of particular articles. The abuse of these grants reached such a pitch in the reign of Queen Elizabeth as to raise great difficulties between the Crown and the House of Commons, till the Queen, alive to the danger of the situation, withdrew the most obnoxious of her grants. In the reign of her successor an Act was passed (21 James I. chap. 3.) declaring all such monopolies to be void, except patents for new inventions. Since that time neither the Government nor Parliament has ever attempted itself to exercise, or to give to other persons by law, an exclusive right of producing or selling anything, except in the case of patents, and of the somewhat similar case of copyright, to which further reference is made below.

In abstaining from granting monopolies the state has also in general abstained from interfering with prices. In the case of labour there are some exceptions to this general rule of abstention on the part of the state. Cab fares, watermen's fares, and pilotage rates, are determined by law, even when the service is not a monopoly, on the ground of simple convenience. The advantages which might arise from the free competition of the open market are not sufficient to counterbalance the annoyance of standing in the street haggling with a cabman, or the grievance of outrageous demands by a local pilot on an ignorant and helpless stranger. But except in such cases as these, and of the special cases mentioned in Chapter X. where circumstances make monopoly inevitable, and where the consumer must consequently be protected against it, I am not aware of any case in which the state prescribes or interferes with the price of an article sold in the ordinary course of trade. Supply and demand are left to determine values and prices. Competition between sellers, and the self-interest of buyers, insures a supply on reasonable terms.

But there are, as I have said, exceptions, and I proceed to consider them.

In two of these instances, those namely of patents and of copyrights, monopolies (I use the word in no invidious sense) are purposely created by the state. In the third instance, that namely of certain joint-stock undertakings, the monopoly is an accident arising not out of the intention of the Legislature, but out of the circumstances of the case.

CHAPTER IX

' *Patents.*—In the case of patents, the right of granting an exclusive right of manufacture and sale was expressly reserved to the crown by the statute 21 James.I. chap. 3., which put an end to all other monopolies.

The prohibition of monopoly which is the main object of the statute is not, under s. 6, to extend to " any letters patent for fourteen years and under, for the sole working and making of new manufactures to the true and first inventor, so that they be not contrary to law nor mischievous to the State by raising prices of commodities, or hurt of trade, or generally inconvenient." The mode of exercising the prerogative of granting patents is now regulated by various statutes, the principal of which is an Act of 1852 (15 and 16 Vict. chap. 83). Under these statutes the first term of fourteen years may in special cases be extended by the Privy Council for a term not exceeding fourteen years beyond the termination of the original patent.

There has been much controversy in recent years upon the principle of the patent law. Many eminent persons have held, that in the present state of science and manufactures, an exclusive right to make and sell any

new invention and improvement operates as a clog to
progress ; that in each manufacture it is well known at
any given moment what are the improvements most
needed ; that hundreds of busy brains are at work to
supply them ; that it is a mere chance whether one
person or another is the first in the field; and that to
give to A to-day an exclusive right for fourteen years to
a thing which B would have discovered to-morrow, is
unjust.　They say further that continuous improvement
in some large and important machine or process which
is being made by the manufacturer, may be impeded or
stopped, if a patentee has got exclusive possession of a
single step or feature which is an essential, though only
a small, part of the whole machine or process, and which
the manufacturer, possibly himself ignorant of the
patent, may never think of patenting himself.

On the other hand, no less eminent men say, that
without patents there would not be sufficient stimulus to
invention ; they say further, that without patents there
would be no sufficient motive for capitalists to take
up and work a new invention, which is apt to be
disliked, because it breaks in upon the practice of the
trade, and renders old plant and old habits useless.　So
important, say they, is this consideration, that if a new
invention were thrown out into the street for anybody
to pick up and use, it would be worth the while of the
public to pick it up and make it the exclusive property
of some one person in order to induce him to make the
effort necessary to bring it into use.　They say farther
that self-interest will always induce a patentee to spread
the use of his patent as much as possible, and that, as a
matter of fact, no improvements are really found to be
hampered or prevented by the existing law.

It would be interesting in the face of these conflicting arguments, to see the patent law tested in some one critical and important case; such, for instance, as that of the electric light. If there should be the litigation which has been threatened on this subject, and if it should prove that some important invention, such as the incandescent carbon lamp, is the exclusive property of some one of the speculative companies who are now competing wildly for the market, it will put the existing law to a severe test.

But whichever of these two arguments is the better, there is no doubt that at the present moment the argument which supports patents is the one which is in favour with the public; and the improvements which are demanded in the patent law, and which will no doubt be effected, are, greater simplicity, and smaller fees. Many would be glad to add greater security, by requiring the state to guarantee, when it grants the patent, either the utility, or the novelty, of the invention, or both; and thus to anticipate and prevent subsequent litigation on these points before a court of law, which, they say, is not so constituted as to possess any adequate knowledge of technical and scientific subjects. This however appears to be more than any government could possibly undertake to do; and the result of attempting any such step would probably be to mislead inventors, to select the wrong inventions, to reject what would be useful, and generally to hamper invention and trade. No government officials can be competent judges either of the value of an invention, or, which is often equally difficult to determine, of its novelty.

They who do not go this length wish to see the

tribunals which try patent cases improved by the addition of technical and scientific elements.

It should be added that the patent law only extends to the United Kingdom. Each British colony has its own separate patent law, and there is at present no international arrangement on the subject of patents.

Copyright, or the exclusive right to make and sell copies, is now a creation of statutes, the effects of which will be found in Sir J. Fitzjames Stephen's Digest attached to the report of the recent Copyright Commission.[1] Speaking generally, it is a right given by the state to authors and artists to prevent other persons during a certain fixed period from making copies and repetitions of their works, so as to give to the authors and artists all the profit that can be made by the exclusive sale of the copies of their works during that period.

The controversies upon this subject have been endless, and are not quite dead yet, one party claiming for the author an absolute, indefeasible, and perpetual right to control the reproduction or imitation of the products of his brain; the other party denying that any such right exists or ought to exist at all. I have attempted to sum up these arguments in an article in the *Fortnightly Review* for December, 1878, and will not repeat them here. The state has in this, as in most other countries, cut the knot by giving the author the exclusive right of reproduction for a certain limited period. In England as regards books, it is either forty-two years from publication, or the life of the author and seven years afterwards, whichever is the longest.

With most European countries copyright treaties have been made under which our authors possess in those

[1] See Parl. Paper, c. 2036, 1878.

countries, and the authors of those countries possess in our country, the same privileges in respect of copyright as the native authors possess. In making these treaties, English authors, or rather perhaps we should say, English copyright owners, have been allowed to retain as against their own books published with their own consent abroad, the same privilege of exclusion from this country which they possessed when all foreign editions were piracies. The result is, so far as I know, perfectly anomalous and unexampled in any other kind of trade. The manufacturer of an English article of trade—for in this connection we must look on a book as a manufacture —is allowed to have, not only the exclusive production of his article, but two or more separate exclusive rights of production in different places, and to prevent what he produces himself at one place from being sold in another place. He is allowed to publish a cheap edition for the foreign market, and to keep that cheap edition out of the English market, which is reserved for the dear edition of the English publisher. If I go abroad I may buy English books published with the consent of the English author by M. Tauchnitz and others at a very moderate price; but I am liable to be treated as a criminal if I bring these books back into my own country. "Cheap English books abroad, dear English books at home," is the motto and result of this system.

But the foreign European market for English books is a comparative trifle. The really serious questions for English authors, and, I may add, indirectly, for English readers also, are those of copyright in the English Colonies and in the United States. Our English copyright law extends in name to the whole of the empire, but it has never been practically enforced in the English-speaking colonies. Those colonies have always refused to take expensive English editions, and in one form or other have always had the benefit of cheap reprints. This has been much complained of; but it is not surprising that a colonist who can buy a cheap American reprint for a few cents, should decline to pay thirty-one shillings for a new novel, or sixteen shillings for an English octavo. There has consequently been a constant struggle, especially with Canada, which has resulted in the establishment of a separate copyright for English books in that colony, under a special law passed for the purpose. The English author can now, besides possessing his imperial copyright, *valeat quantum*, in Canada, obtain copyright in that country under a Canadian Act; and he can, as in the case of books which he publishes in a foreign European country, exclude from England the edition he publishes in Canada. The author and the Canadian reader get the benefit of the wider market and the cheaper prices, but the native Englishman is excluded from them.

Still more important is the market of the United States. That country has hitherto refused to enter into any copyright treaty at all. The great publishers of her Eastern Cities have up to a recent period had the market in their own hands; they have reprinted English books, giving such remuneration as they pleased to the author; and have by arrangement between themselves abstained from pirating from one another. But the Union grows rapidly, and with it the demand for, and the supply of books. Publishers have grown up in the western and southern cities who publish their own cheap editions of popular English books with as little regard to New York and Boston as New York and Boston have hitherto paid to Paternoster Row. The consequence is that the great eastern publishers have recently found their interest in promoting some form of international copyright law by which they should, whilst retaining the privilege of re-manufacturing English books in America, be protected against western and southern piracies, and there has consequently been some talk of a copyright treaty on this basis. But this talk has come to nothing, as indeed was to be expected, since it left out of account the most important interest of all, viz., that of the great American reading public.

It cannot be too often or too strongly urged that the great obstacle to all arrangements with our own colonies and with the United States, by which our authors might reap the full benefit of an extended market, is the high price at which first editions are published in this country. A standard octavo volume, which costs perhaps about 3s. 4d. in print, paper and binding,[1] is published at 16s. Till this practice of the trade is altered, English-speaking communities across the Atlantic will refuse to put themselves into the fetters of a copyright law. There are symptoms of better things. Many books, especially those having something of a scientific or educational character, are published, copyright or no copyright, at moderate prices on both sides the Atlantic, and cheap editions of popular works in this country are becoming earlier and more frequent. The time may come when a 16s. octavo, or a 31s. novel, may appear as much out of date as the quartos in which our fathers and grandfathers

---

[1] These were the figures, which, after careful inquiry, I laid before the Copyright Commission; and which, I believe, present a fair average of cost, though it is of course very different in different cases.

read their first editions of *Marmion* or of the *Decline and Fall*.

In every other branch of English trade and manufacture, the principle which has led to such magnificent results both for manufacturer and consumer, is that of numerous dealings with small profits on each dealing, and there is no reason why the same principle should not be equally true and effective in the case of books. The English-speaking and reading community is enormous, and is growing as no other community grows. It ought to give to English authors such remuneration as literature has never yet received, and to readers lower prices than have ever yet been paid for books, and it must be the fault of bad laws or bad habits if this is not the case. In any future arrangements with our Colonies or with the United States, it is to be hoped that this great end may be kept in view, and that the different interests concerned, viz., the interests of authors, of publishers, and of the reading public in both countries, may all and each receive full and fair consideration ; and that no one of these interests, least of all that of the readers in this country, may be sacrificed to the interest, real or supposed, of any other class. That they are really the same at bottom, and that the interests of all will be best consulted by the utmost possible freedom compatible with a copyright law, I fully believe.

CHAPTER X.

ACTION OF THE STATE IN THE MATTER OF CERTAIN
UNDERTAKINGS WHICH ARE TOTAL OR PARTIAL
MONOPOLIES.

THERE is a large and constantly increasing class of industrial undertakings, possessing privileges which give them more or less the character of monopolies, and which thus call for special regulation by the state. It is a matter of speculative interest to ascertain what these undertakings are, and what are the characteristics which they possess in common, so that we may be able to recognise and define them. It is a matter of more practical interest to examine what steps have been taken by the state to regulate them, and with what success.

General Character of these Undertakings.—It would be difficult and probably fruitless to attempt to determine the character of these undertakings *à priori* or by way of deduction. The more satisfactory plan is to take the several undertakings in detail, to ascertain their several characteristics, and then to examine the manner in which they have been dealt with.

The following is a tolerably complete list of these undertakings :—Harbours and natural navigations, canals, docks, lighthouses, roads, bridges and ferries, railways, tramways, gasworks, waterworks, the post-office, and telegraphs.

In some of these, *e.g.* docks, railways, gasworks and telegraphs, competition has been attempted; whilst others have been monopolies from their commencement.

But in none of them has competition proved to be completely successful. It is of great importance that this point should be kept steadily in view, since it is only in those cases which competition cannot fully regulate, and so far as competition does not regulate them, that the need for special state interference is felt.

Is there, then, any general characteristic by which these undertakings, or others of a similar kind, may be recognised and distinguished from undertakings which are governed by the ordinary law of competition.

It is not *large capital*, for though most of them require large capital, some gas and water companies, which are complete monopolies, have capitals of not more than two or three thousand pounds; whilst other enterprises, with enormous capitals, *e.g.* banks, insurance offices, shipping companies, are not monopolies.

It is not *positive law*, for few of them have a monopoly expressly granted or confirmed by law; and in most, if not all, of the cases where such a monopoly happens to have been so granted or confirmed, it would have existed without such grant or confirmation.

They all agree in *supplying necessaries*. But this alone is no test, for butchers and bakers supply necessaries.

Most, if not all, of them have *exclusive possession or occupation of certain peculiarly favourable portions of land,*—*e.g.* docks, of the river-side; gas and water companies, of the streets. But this is only true in a limited sense of such undertakings as the post-office, telegraphs, or even of roads and railways ; and a mine, a quarry, or a fishery, has equally possession of specially favoured sites without generally or necessarily becoming a monopoly.

The article or convenience supplied by them is *local*, and cannot be dissevered from the possession or user of the land or premises occupied by the undertaking. The undertaking does not produce an article to be carried away and sold in a distant market, but a convenience in the use of the undertaking itself, as in the case of harbours, roads, railways, post-office, and telegraphs ; or an article sold and used on the spot where it is produced, as in the case of gas and water.

Again, in most of these cases the convenience afforded or article produced is one which can be *increased almost indefinately*, without proportionate increase of the original plant ; so that to set up a rival scheme is an extravagant waste of capital.

There is also in some of these undertakings, and notoriously in the cases of the post-office, of telegraphs, and of railways, another consideration, viz., the paramount importance of *certainty and harmonious arrangement*. In the case of most industries— *e.g.* in that of a baker—it would be easier to know what to do if there were one instead of several to choose from ; but this consideration is in such a case not paramount to considerations of cheapness. In the case of the post-office and telegraphs, certainty and harmony are the paramount considerations. The inconvenience would be extreme if we had to consider and choose the mode of conveyance every time a letter is despatched, or if a telegram sent from any one station could not be despatched to all other stations.

The following then appear to be the characteristics of undertakings which tend to become monopolies :—

1. What they supply is a necessary.

2. They occupy peculiarly favoured spots or lines of land.

3. The article or convenience they supply is used at the place where and in connection with the plant or machinery by which it is supplied.

4. This article or convenience can in general be largely, if not indefinitely increased, without proportionate increase in plan and capital.

5. Certainty and harmonious arrangement, which can only be attained by unity, are paramount considerations.

Mode of dealing with them.—The above conclusions are neither as clear nor as complete as could be wished. And though interesting in a speculative point of view, they do not lead immediately to any important practical consequence. But the further question in what manner these undertakings are dealt with—in what manner— that is to say—the state endeavours to counteract the evils of monopoly or privilege is a question of great practical interest, and one with which we are directly concerned here.

There are two great alternatives.

(1.) Ownership and management by private enterprise and capital under regulation by the state.

(2.) Ownership and management by Government, central or local.

In the former I include all cases in which those who undertake the work derive personal gain from capital which they invest in it ; and in the latter all cases, whether of management by the central government, by municipal bodies, by local boards, or by public trusts or commissions, generally elective, in which no private capital is invested, except by way of loan, and no profit made by individuals.

Before entering in any detail upon the examination of these two alternatives, it will be interesting to see how they have been regarded by competent authorities in this country and in France respectively. The following are Mr. Mill's observations on this subject (*Political Economy*, vol ii. chap. xi. s. 11) :—

"The third exception which I shall notice to the doctrine that government cannot manage the affairs of individuals as well as the individuals themselves, has reference to the great class of cases in which the individuals can only manage the concern by delegated agency, and in which the so-called private management is, in point of fact, hardly better entitled to be called management by the persons interested, than administration by a public officer. Whatever, if left to spontaneous agency, can only be done by joint-stock associations, will often be as well, and sometimes better done, as far as the actual work is concerned, by the state. Government management is, indeed, proverbially jobbing, careless, and ineffective ; but so likewise has generally been joint-stock management. The directors of a joint-stock company, it is true, are always shareholders ; but also the members of a government are invariably taxpayers ; and in the case of directors, no more than in that of governments, is their proportional share of the benefits of good management, equal to the interest they may possibly have in mis-management, even without reckoning the interest of their case. It may be objected, that the shareholders, in their collective character, exercise a certain control over the directors, and have almost always full power to remove them from office. Practically, however, the difficulty of exercising

this power is found to be so great, that it is hardly ever
exercised except in cases of such flagrantly unskilful,
or, at least, unsuccessful management, as would generally produce the ejection from office of managers
appointed by the government.   Against the security
afforded by meetings of shareholders, and by their
individual inspection and inquiries, may be placed the
greater publicity and more active discussion and com-
ment, to be expected in free countries with regard to
affairs in which the general government takes part.
The defects, therefore, of government management, do
not seem to be necessarily much greater, if necessarily
greater at all, than those of management by joint-stock.
   " The true reasons in favour of leaving to voluntary
associations all such things as they are competent to
perform, would exist in equal strength if it were certain
that the work itself would be as well or better done by
public officers.   These reasons have been already pointed-
out : the mischief of overloading the chief functionaries
of government with demands on their attention, and
diverting them from duties which they alone can discharge, to objects which can be sufficiently well attained
without them : the danger of unnecessarily swelling the
direct power and indirect influence of government, and
multiplying occasions of collision between its agents and
private citizens ; and the still greater inexpediency of
concentrating in a dominant bureaucracy, all the skill
and experience in the management of large interests,
and all the power of organised action, existing in the
community : a practice which keeps the citizens in a
relation to the government like that of children to
their guardians, and is a main cause of the inferior
capacity for political life which has hitherto character-
ised the over governed countries of the Continent,
whether with or without the forms of representative
government.
   " But although, for these reasons, most things which
are likely to be even tolerably done by voluntary associations, should, generally speaking, be left to them, it
does not follow that the manner in which those associ-

ations perform their work should be entirely uncontrolled by the government. There are many cases in which the agency, of whatever nature, by which a service is performed, is certain, from the nature of the case, to be virtually single ; in which a practical monopoly, with all the power it confers of taxing the community, cannot be prevented from existing. I have already more than once adverted to the case of the gas and water companies, among which, though perfect freedom is allowed to competition, none really takes place, and practically they are found to be even more irresponsible and unapproachable by individual complaints than the government. There are the expenses without the advantages of plurality of agency ; and the charge made for services which cannot be dispensed with, is, in substance, quite as much compulsory taxation as if imposed by law : there are few householders who make any distinction between their ' water rate ' and their other local taxes. In the case of these particular services the reasons preponderate in favour of their being performed, like the paving and cleansing of the streets, not certainly by the general government of the state, but by the municipal authorities of the town, and the expense defrayed as even now it in fact is by a local rate. But in the many analogous cases which it is best to resign to voluntary agency, the community needs some other security for the fit performance of the service than the interest of the managers ; and it is part of the government either to subject the business to reasonable conditions for the general advantage, or to retain such power over it that the profits of the monopoly may at least be obtained for the public. This applies to the case of a road, a canal, or a railway. These are always, in a great degree, practical monopolies ; and a government which concedes such monopoly unreservedly to a private company, does much the same thing as if it allowed an individual or an association to levy any tax they chose for their own benefit on all the malt produced in the country, or on all the cotton imported into it. To make the concession for a limited time is generally justifiable, on the principle which justifies patents for inventions; but the state should either reserve to itself a reversionary property in such public works, or should retain, and freely exercise, the right of fixing a maximum of fares and charges, and from time to time, varying that maximum. It is perhaps necessary to remark, that the state may be the proprietor of canals or railways without itself working them; and that they will 'almost always be better worked by means of a company renting the railway or canal for a limited period from the state."

The following is an extract from an article on monopolies in the French *Dictionnaire d'Économie Politique.* (Coquelin et Guillaumin, Paris, 1854, vol. ii., *art. Monopolies,* p. 224):—

"In France the initiative and direction of these works (*i.e.* harbours, internal navigations, roads, bridges, railways) belongs to the central authority, acting by by means of a numerous and expensive body, the engineers of roads and bridges (*ingénieurs des ponts et chaussées*). Most of the great channels of communication are established at the cost of the public, according to the schemes or designs of these engineering officials; the schemes which are started independently of them are subjected to their control; and it scarcely ever happens that such schemes are accepted by the authorities against their advice. The result of this *régime* is, that in respect of works of this character the spirit of enterprise is wholly discouraged, and that scarcely anything is accomplished except at the instance and by the impulse of the body of official engineers, an impulse which, for reasons which we have given under the title 'Fonctionnaires,' is incomparably less powerful and less fertile than that of free industry. Thus, none of the great improvements in artificial channels of communication or in means of transport which have been introduced within the last fifty years, have originated in France—macadamisation of roads, railroads, locomotives, suspension bridges, steamboats, &c., all are the work of the free and independent engineers of England or America. The monopoly of our official engineers is as little adapted to improve and utilise inventions as to start them. And although our country is one of those in which industry is most highly developed, and in which a multiplicity of the most perfect channels of communication—*e.g.*, of railways—is the most necessary, we have remained in this respect far behind the United States, England, Belgium, &c. A further result of the French system is that the channels of communication are distributed over the country without any real proportion to the wants of its several districts, and that their expense, instead of being supported, as in England, by tolls levied on those who use them, and in proportion to the use they make of them, falls without reference to the service rendered, on all contributors alike."

It is obvious that the two writers have been influenced in the above observations by the different modes in which these enterprises have been developed in the two countries. The English philosopher has been struck by the evils arising from the English practice of granting unrestricted monopolies to private persons. The French writer, on the other hand, has been more alive to the want of enterprise which has followed upon the French practice of leaving such undertakings to be originated by government. The observations of both writers are undoubtedly just, each from his own point of view; and any consideration of the subject is imperfect which does not take both elements into full consideration.

Shortly stated, the following are the arguments in

favour of government or public management, and they are no doubt extremely strong :—

1. Joint-stock management, as Mr. Mill points out, has by no means the advantages in energy and self-interest over public government which enterprises managed by individuals have.

2. There is greater unity in management and certainty in use.

3. The public get the benefit of any profit, either in reduction of price or in relief of taxation ; consequently the interests of the producers and consumers is the same, and there is not the same temptation either to excessive charges or to needless investment of capital, as there is in the case of joint-stock companies.

On the other hand, we must not forget that if joint-stock companies have some of the disadvantages, they have also some of the advantages of government management. The chairman and officers of some of the great joint-stock companies have a pride in the well-doing of their undertaking similar to that of a public administrator, or a zealous town clerk. Again, government management is proverbially sluggish, and is open to parliamentary and municipal jobbing. It is also liable to be influenced by sentiment and impulse rather than by a cool consideration of the wants to be supplied, and thus is not unlikely to select wrong fields for its energy.

But a far more important argument against committing all these undertakings to government is, that capital will find its own way and do what is wanted ; and government, whether general or local, will not.

This is principally due to the activity which individuals display in seeking their own profit as compared with the sluggishness of public governing bodies. To this action of individual interest special circumstances have in the course of the last and the present centuries largely contributed. The history of personal rights and property has, as Sir H. S. Maine tells us, been one of constant development, and, in earlier periods of our history, the community, as compared with the individual, played a larger part than at present. Accordingly, the earliest of the undertakings we are speaking of, *e.g.*, the maintenance and improvement of our natural harbours and navigations, and the oldest of our roads and bridges, were originally managed by public bodies. Towards the end of last century and the beginning of this, various circumstances contributed to effect a change. In public opinion, and in the eye of the law, the weight attached to personal rights had become greater. Political economy taught the superior energy of individual enterprise. Capital accumulated and was seeking investment. Our laws of partnership, too, were altered, so as to enable the capital of many individuals to be united for a single purpose. And, lastly, engineering science made gigantic strides, and opened out the way for industrial undertakings such as the world had never seen before. Hence, for the last hundred years, the current has set in the direction of private enterprise, and by this means the country has been supplied with necessaries and conveniences which public management would never have afforded.

Of late there has been somewhat of a reaction ; there is now a disposition to strengthen and improve local and municipal institutions, and to invest them with wider functions. It seems probable, too, that this

movement will increase.   But it will be long before it
does for us what private enterprise has done and is
doing.

There are too, certain enterprises for which it is
peculiarly unfitted, enterprises namely which involve
scientific experiment, and which depend for their
financial success upon the results of those experiments.
Such enterprises are necessarily speculative, and it is
undesirable for many obvious reasons that a Government, whether of a country or of a town should embark
upon them.   A government ought not to seek excessive
profit, or run the risk of serious loss.   A government
is, from the nature of its organization, peculiarly unfitted to display the flexibility and the facility of
resource necessary for successful experiments.   The
failure of a speculation in the hands of private persons
is a mere private loss.   The failure of a speculation in
the hands of a government is an injury to its character.
For these reasons it is not desirable that a government,
whether general or local, should take upon itself any
description of trade, manufacture, or service, until
the process to be employed has been ascertained by
experience, and until the financial success of the undertaking and the conditions under which it can be carried
on are determined and known.

Whilst, however, private enterprise has done so
much for us, it must be admitted that there has been
little thought or foresight about the ultimate results of
the huge monopolies we have been creating.   The few
conditions by which Parliament has sought to restrict
them have often been useless, and, occasionally, worse
than useless.

These general observations will be best illustrated

and supported by a glance at the history of the several undertakings to which we have referred.

1. *Harbours and Natural Navigations.*—The improvement of these were among the first of large public works. They originated before the era of joint-stock companies, and, with the exception of a few small harbours owned by large landowners, are, and always have been, in the hands of some public body, *i.e.*, either of a municipal corporation, or a public trust, or commission, and not of profit-making companies.

An evil of considerable magnitude has arisen in cases where the public body exercising this power is no longer the representative of the trade which uses the harbour, as, for instance, where the town of Liverpool owned the Liverpool docks. In such cases the locality is too apt to tax the trade of the country for its own benefit. But even in cases such as these, the sea—greatest of free traders—generally limits the growth of the evil. If taxes are too high at one port, ships can, in most cases, seek another.

2. *Canals.*—These were amongst the first products of the new engineering era, and have been, and now are, almost entirely in the hands of joint-stock companies. They have, however, been generally superseded or swallowed up by railways, and are now of comparatively little importance. But for this we should probably have heard many complaints of their profits and charges.

At the present moment there is a movement in their favour, and an attempt to set them up again as rivals to railways. For certain classes of goods where speed is of no importance they may yet be useful; and they have the advantage of being roads on which all carriers can compete. But the total inadequacy of the existing canal system to the present traffic of the country : the difficulty of extending it ; and the impossibility of carrying upon it with the speed which modern trade requires—not to mention the fact that half the existing canals are in the hands of railway companies, all render it impossible to look to the system of internal canals as more than a subsidiary mode of conveyance.

3. *Docks* were also an early product of the engineering era, and, consequently, they were often made in the first instance by private capital. From the limited area in each port available for docks, they are often, so far as the port itself is concerned, complete monopolies. But the sea, as we have said, is the greatest of free traders. The rivalry of other ports generally prevents any very bad effect from a dock monopoly, and rouses the trade of the port to put a stop to it when it becomes oppressive. Partly for this reason, and partly because it has been found that rivalry in the same port between competing dock and harbour authorities creates confusion, difficulty, quarrels, and expense, whilst harmonious arrangement is of paramount importance to trade, the tendency for the last twenty years has been to hand over the management and construction of docks to local trusts representing the whole interests of the port and making no profit. Thus docks made by private companies at Sunderland, Liverpool, and Birkenhead, have been in late years handed over to public trusts ; whilst at Newcastle and Shields, at Glasgow and Greenock, at Dundee, Leith, Belfast, and Aberdeen, and other ports, docks recently made have been constructed and are managed by public bodies representing the dock ratepayers.

4. *Lighthouses* have now, for some years, been made by the governments of all civilised countries. But in England, which was the first to build them, many of them were originally granted by the Crown to private persons with power to take tolls: and it is only since 1830 that the lighthouses so granted have been bought up and placed under public control. Even now the coasts of Turkey are lighted by a French joint-stock company, and there are complaints of its charges and of the profits it is said to be making.

On the proper mode of managing lighthouses there is little to be said. It is admitted on all hands that they must be in the hands of a central authority, and ought not to be a matter of profit to private persons. Whether they should be paid for in the shape of tolls on ships, or by the public exchequer, does not seem to be a question raising any important issue of economical principle. In both cases they are paid for more or less directly by the general consumer; in the one case, through the medium of freights—in the other, more directly by general taxation. The former plan has the practical advantage of affording a good test of the value of any proposed new works, in the willingness or unwillingness of the shipping interest, who are the immediate payers, to saddle themselves with the necessary tolls.

5. *Roads.*—These were originally made by the local authority, *i.e.* by the parish. But under the demand for channels of through communication to be used by wheeled vehicles, and with the engineering improvements of the last century, the system of turnpike trusts grew up, a system under which private capital was obtained in the shape of loans secured upon tolls, and

the management placed in the hands of a body of trustees, partly public, partly private. The tendency of late years has been to do away with this system—to improve highway boards—to place the whole of the roads under their management—to abolish turnpike tolls, and to pay expenses out of rates. The importance of turnpike trusts is diminishing yearly—partly for the above reason, partly on account of the transfer of through traffic to railways. The number of turnpike trusts, in England and Wales, according to the last published return,[1] was 248; their income £218,478, and their capital debt £581,080—a mere flea-bite compared with joint-stock company capital—and annually decreasing.

The mileage of roads in England and Wales maintained out of rates is 115,773; the income £1,929,310, and the expenditure £1,895,001.[2]

Under these circumstances the management of roads calls for no special observation. Turnpike tolls are a nuisance; but they are in a fair way to be abolished, and all the roads in the kingdom are likely soon to be in the hands of local authorities and supported by local rates. One effect of the change seems likely to be that the old turnpike roads or through channels of traffic will be less well kept up than they were under the old system, whilst the more local roads and cross roads, in which the local managers are interested, will be improved.

6. *Bridges and Ferries.*—These form part of roads, and have been similarly dealt with, except in certain special cases, such as the bridges over the Thames,

---

[1] Parl. Paper, C.—2966 of 1881.
[2] Parl. Paper, C.—3274 of 1882.

which, as we know, have been originally built by private enterprise on the security of tolls, and which are now gradually being bought up by public bodies. It is not likely that many more bridges will be constructed on this principle. But if they are, it is obviously desirable that the concession should be for a limited term, and that in no case should it be accompanied, as has too often been the case, with a prohibition to set up another bridge or ferry within a certain distance, which, of course, has the effect of conferring a strict legal monopoly.

7. *Railways.*—These have all been made since the setting in of the engineering and joint-stock era, and are in the hands of joint-stock companies. They are the great example, for good and for evil, of the joint-stock system. The subject of railways alone, if exhaustively treated, would far exceed the limits of this treatise. It is so important that I have made it the subject of a separate chapter,[1] and only refer to it here.

8. *Tramways.*—These are almost a comparatively new enterprise, and the legislature in dealing with this subject has had the benefit of the experience of the difficulties which have been felt in the case of railway and gas and water companies. By the General Tramways Act,[2] 1870, Parliament gave to the municipal authorities facilities for constructing tramways themselves, in priority to companies, and for charging the expenses on rates; whilst it also subjected the concessions which might be made to tramway companies to new and unprecedented conditions.

In the first place, the concession is not to be made to a company if the municipal authority chooses to under-

---

[1] See Chap. XII.   [2] 33 & 34 Vict. c. 78.

take the work; and then only with the consent of the municipal authority, and under such conditions as it may impose. When the tramway is opened, if it is not so worked as to give the public the full benefit of it, licences to use it on payment of certain tolls may be granted to other persons by the Board of Trade. When the promoting company have had the use of the tramway for twenty-one years, the municipal authority may purchase it at the then actual value of the permanent plant, without any payment in respect of profits or compensation for compulsory sale, such value to be fixed by a Government referee.

According to the Parliamentary return for 1881 [1] the total number of tramway undertakings authorised under this act is 122. The capital authorised is £10,906,575, the capital expended £6,939,285, and the number of miles open 488. The number of these undertakings made by municipal authorities is 24, with an authorised capital of £1,787,462 and an expended capital of £1,075,686. The number made by joint-stock companies is 98, with an authorised capital of £9,119,113, and an expended capital of £5,864,152. This shows how active private capital is in promoting new undertakings when compared with representative governing bodies.

9. *Gas-Works.*—The case of gas supply is peculiar, since gas manufacture has reached a high state of development and success; and the complete effect of the attempts Parliament has made to control the monopoly is better seen than in cases where profits are still small. In many cases the dividends have become so large that the public are painfully aware of the conflict of interest

[1] Parl. Paper 404 of 1881.

between themselves and the shareholders ; and, on the other hand, in certain large places, prudent municipalities have made a good thing for the ratepayers out of the supply of gas.

There is one case—viz., Manchester—in which the gas-works have been originally established by the municipality, and there may be others. There are many cases in which works originally established by a company have been subsequently bought by the municipality, and these cases are on the increase ; but how few they are, in comparison to the cases of gas-works still owned by companies, may be seen from the following figures. The total number of gas companies in England and Wales, according to the Parliamentary return [1] of 1881, is 336, with an aggregate authorised capital of about £41,500,000. In the metropolis there are four gas companies, with a capital of £13,000,000.[2] Besides these, there are a certain number of public gas-works in the hands of private persons ; and against this number of private enterprises there are 136 cases in which the municipal authority is the owner of the gas-works.

The history of gas supply is so instructive that it is worth while to give some details concerning it. When gas was first introduced the manufacture was a novelty and a risk ; and even now it is an expensive thing to establish gas-works where the population is small and scattered. But the manufacture improves, and costs less and less in proportion to the supply as it gets larger ; whilst, as population grows, there is an increased demand. Consequently, prices which are just when the concern begins become too large after a few years, and

[1] Parl. Paper 315 of 1881.
[2] Parl. Paper 259 of 1882.

then begins a struggle between the consumers and the companies. In London, an attempt was made to meet this by competition; and for some years the streets were pulled up by rival companies endeavouring to outbid each other. This was found to be such a nuisance that London was " districted " between the companies by Act of Parliament, thus giving each of them a legal monopoly. The districts allotted to the several companies were determined, not so much by the wants of the town as by the circumstances of the companies; and the consequence is that there has been until lately an extravagant division and distribution of manufacture and supply. Amalgamation has however been encouraged by recent legislation, and in London there are, or shortly will be, only two great companies, one north and the other south of the Thames.

Under the General Act of 1847,[1] there are no provisions for testing the power and quality of gas supplied to the consumer; those contained in the London Act of 1860,[2] proved ineffectual; and more effectual provisions were introduced, by the Act of 1868,[3] and subsequent Acts. This is a matter in which the difficulty is of a technical rather than of a financial or economical character, and the attempts to meet it have been attended with some success. This is more than can be said of most of the attempts which have been made to control price. Until recently the main, and almost the only, condition on which the legislature has relied for preventing the public from being placed at the mercy of the gas companies was its favourite panacea of limiting profits. It was provided by the General Act

[1] 10 & 11 Vict. cap. 15.
[2] 23 & 24 Vict. cap. 125.   [3] 31 & 32 Vict. cap. 125.

concerning gas companies that each company was to be satisfied with a 10 per cent. dividend, besides making up past dividends to 10 per cent. and setting aside a reserve fund to secure future dividends at the same rate ; and that if any company divided more than this amount of profit, a court of justice might reduce the price of gas to such an amount as would bring down their profits to the above limit.

Now, in the first place, to suppose that any court of justice can constitute itself a judge of the price which will produce a certain profit and no more, is absurd ; and the more elaborate provisions of some of the recent London gas acts, which intrusted this delicate operation to more competent hands, have proved a failure also. No Government department, or scientific commission appointed by Government, can undertake to say to a manufacturer, "At such and such a price you can manufacture an article which shall produce you exactly 10 per cent. dividend—no more, and no less." To do this requires all the knowledge, skill, and constant experience of the manufacturer himself ; and no one but himself can tell what capital he needs, what expenses he must incur, and what economies he can practise.

But further, the principle of limitation of dividend is in itself faulty. So long as the charge is not too high, the public have no interest in the reduction of dividend. Their interest is in the reduction of price, which is a totally different thing. If the consumer can get his gas at 2s. instead of 4s. per 1000 cubic feet, he is not the less benefited if the shareholder at the same time gets 20 per cent. instead of 10 per cent. The fallacy lies in supposing that what is taken from the shareholder necessarily goes into the pocket of the consumer.

It does no such thing; it is probably wasted in staff
and other easy extravagances, which the company have
no motive whatever for reducing. Indeed one of the
worst consequences of the system is, that it takes away
from the manufacturer (who it is to be remembered is a
monopolist) his last and only inducement to improvement and economy. It leads not only to extravagance
in current expenses, but to an extravagant waste of
capital. The shareholder having an easy and safe 10
per cent. on his original shares, is naturally anxious to
invest more money on so good a security, and is only
too glad if he can find an excuse for a further outlay.
Parliament, it is true, gives now only 7 per cent. on
fresh capital, and pretends to ascertain by investigation
before a select committee whether more capital is
wanted. This, again, is a question which neither a
committee nor a department of government can satisfactorily determine. No one but the manufacturer
himself can say with any certainty how much capital he
needs; and Parliament, pressed by the argument that,
if the company is not allowed to invest more capital
the town will not be lighted, cannot help giving to a
company the power of investing large sums which might
well be spared, and the interest of which becomes a
totally unnecessary charge on consumers of gas.

In fact, in this Parliamentary limitation of dividend
and capital we have gone on a perfectly wrong tack and
have involved ourselves in a maze of absurdities·
Coupled with the statutory price of gas, it really
operates as a guarantee to the companies of an easy
10 per cent. dividend.

But Parliament was not content with this encouragement to extravagance. In its anxiety to regulate the

internal financial concerns of the companies, which they were perfectly able to manage for themselves, it required them to offer all new capital to the existing shareholders at par. As the capital with a safe 10 per cent. dividend was worth twice its nominal amount, this was in effect giving to the shareholders out of the pockets of the consumers £200 for each £100 of new capital which they provided, and of course operated as an inducement to them to spend as much new capital as possible. It is scarcely possible that State interference could have been more mischievous.

These abuses have to some extent been modified, if not put an end to, by recent legislation. As regards profits, a sliding scale of price and dividend has been adopted, under which, starting from a given point of price and dividend, the gas companies are enabled for every penny per thousand feet by which they reduce the price of gas, to add a quarter per cent. to their dividend, so as to divide any additional profit they may make between the companies and their consumers. This plan not only gives the consumer a share in increased profits, but also gives the companies a motive for economy. It has been adopted in London and in many other towns.

As regards capital, gas companies coming to Parliament for power to raise money are required to put up to auction all the fresh capital they require, so that any premium upon the shares goes into the plant and stock of the company, and not into the pockets of the shareholders.

Both of these provisions seem to have worked well. The sliding scale is adopted in fifty-two, the auction clauses in 104, places. Both are adopted in London.

As I have already stated, a still more complete solution of the gas difficulty has been found in several large towns, where the town councils have either made or purchased the gas-works. In Manchester, where they have for many years owned the gas-works, the result is, that after supplying good gas at a cheap rate they have, and have long had, a surplus of from £40,000 to £50,000 a year, with which they have effected all the recent numerous and expensive improvements in the town, besides paying a large part of the cost of their still more expensive water-works. In the twenty years ending with 1870 they had, after paying the current expenses of gas manufacture and supply, made more than a million of surplus profits. This mode of dealing with the question has received countenance from recent general legislature. By the Public Health Act urban authorities are authorised to supply gas, though only in places where there is no existing gas company.

10. *Electric Lighting.*—On this subject it is too early yet to speak of results. But some important principles have been established by the Act passed last session (45 & 46 Vict. ch. 56). It has been determined by that Act that gas companies have no monopoly and no priority in respect of light, but only in respect of gas; and it is evident that the competition to which they are now exposed is already producing its effects in the improvement of gas. It has further been determined that municipalities shall have the priority in providing electricity if they choose to do it themselves; that they shall have a veto on the seven years licences which the Board of Trade are enabled, with their consent, to grant to private companies, and that when they refuse their assent, concessions to companies can only be made by

provisional order of the Board of Trade confirmed by Parliament. A still more important provision is one (s. 27) which, following the precedent of the Tramways Act, provides that after twenty-one years the local authority of the district may purchase the undertaking compulsorily on the terms of paying to the company the then value of all land, buildings, and plant. belonging to the company, at their then market value, having regard to their condition and their suitability to the purpose of the undertaking, but without any addition for compulsory purchase, goodwill, or future profits.

This is a case in which the enterprise is still of a speculative and experimental character ; and therefore, if the remarks made in an earlier part of this chapter are sound, it is not one which it is desirable for municipal governments to take into their own hands or to manipulate themselves. If they do so, they run the risk of discrediting both the enterprise itself and the character of local government. Whether they become in form the undertakers, and then employ private companies to undertake the speculation under their control, or allow private companies to become the undertakers themselves, it is pretty certain that the real pioneering must be done by private capital, and that the governing bodies of the towns will not become the manufacturers of electricity till the process is better understood than it is now. In making arrangements with the companies the final interest of the public will in any case be protected by the ultimate power to buy up the monopoly, and it is to the interest of the public that the companies should make a fair profit in the meantime. Indeed the existence of gas, and the competition with it, is of itself sufficient to prevent for the present any excessive and exorbitant price being demanded for electric lighting.

11. *Water Supply.*—In many respects this is like gas supply. But water differs in being even more necessary, in being more difficult to procure, and in requiring greater outlay, with less profit, as the demand increases. The supply also requires greater precautions to prevent waste—precautions which it is difficult to intrust to a private company. Under these circumstances, recently established water companies, though not unprofitable, have been less profitable than gas companies; and their differences with the consumer have related to deficiency and impurity in the supply as much as to price. Probably none of them, certainly none of the London companies, pay 10 per cent. on recent investments.

Under these circumstances, the number of municipalities which have supplied themselves with water is greater than in the case of gas. The number of water companies in the United Kingdom, exclusive of London, as given in the published lists some years since was about 120, with a capital of between £7,000,000, and £8,000,000. In London there are eight companies, with a capital of more than £12,000,000. On the other hand, there are many undertakings in the hands of municipal authorities; and these are to be found in many of the largest towns, *e.g.* Liverpool, Manchester, and Glasgow.

The regulations to which Parliament has subjected water companies [1] are almost the same as in the case of gas.

As regards limitation of profits, the conditions are

___

[1] Water-works Clauses Act, 10 & 11 Vict. c. 17.

precisely the same; but their ultimate effect is not so well seen, because the limit has seldom been reached.

It is needless to refer to the well-known case of the London water companies and the attempt to purchase them. It is a good illustration of the evil of an unlimited concession of a monopoly of a necessary of life to a private company, and of the difficulty of retracing false steps.

In this case, still more than in that of gas, it is important for the health of the people that the supply should be in the hands of a body which can have no motive for restricting it; which does not seek profit from it; which can enforce rules for preventing waste, and which can draw upon other funds, if the expense of supply is large.

Parliament has consequently by the Public Health Act 1875, given to local authorities ample powers to supply water to the inhabitants of their district, not only when there is no water company, but where the supply by an existing company is improper or insufficient.

12. *Post-Office and Telegraphs.*—This, which is a most striking instance of a trading government monopoly, is so important that I have made it the subject of a separate chapter.[1]

Conclusions.—From the above notice of these several undertakings, we may draw the following conclusions of fact:—

(1.) That in an earlier state of society, the undertakings of which we are speaking were generally established and maintained by some public governing body, whether of the country generally, of the districts or interests concerned.

[1] See Chap. XI.

(2.) That at a later period private capital and enterprise came to the assistance of Government, and did, and still do, what Government never could or would have done.

(3.) That at a later period still, the evils arising from placing these undertakings, which must be to some extent monopolies, in the hands of private companies, has been felt; and that there is a tendency again to place many of them in the hands of some public body—central or local.

(4.) That whilst harbours, natural navigations, many docks, roads, and bridges, a few gas-works, some water-works, the post-office, and telegraphs, are now in the hands of the State or of local governing bodies, many docks, all railways, most tramways, and most gas and water-works, are in the hands of private companies; and further, that the capital invested in these private undertakings amounts probably to £1,000,000,000.

(5.) That there are many points in which the interests of these companies are at variance with those of the public; and that the conditions which the state has imposed on them for the purpose of preventing their monopoly from being injurious to the public are still tentative; that these remedies have often proved inadequate, and sometimes mischievous; and that whilst it is right and necessary to impose some restrictions on them, yet without great caution and wisdom such restrictions are likely to be injurious to the public as well as to the companies.

(6.) That the endeavour to get local authorities to undertake these works themselves, and where concessions are made to private companies to limit them in point of time, as has been done in the case of tramways and electric lighting, though as yet experimental only, is a hopeful experiment.

The above considerations are economical. There is one other consideration of great importance, but of importance in a political rather than in an economical point of view, viz., the effect which would be produced on the political morals of the country, of a town, or of a district, if the patronage and other opportunities for jobbing involved in the management of large public works were placed in the hands of its governing body. Some evils might thus arise. But most, if not all, of the services in question will be rendered to the public, and in public, and every defect in the service will be promptly noticed and complained of. There is nothing like plenty of work and full publicity for preventing jobbery and keeping administration sound and pure. On the other hand, also, there is a serious political evil to be apprehended from the growing influence of the great joint-stock company interest in Parliament and in local governing boards. This evil is, if report speaks truth, a very serious one in America. In this country it is as yet not much felt, except in the combined resistance which the companies make to any alteration of the law which affects themselves. But the success and ability with which they can do this is, considering the ever-widening sphere of their operations, a great evil in itself, and if they should ever turn their powerful organisation to a political purpose, it would become a national calamity.

Other Cases of Government Supply.—The above are not the only cases in which the State, as represented by local public bodies, has undertaken to supply commodities which are generally left to private enterprise.

By a variety of acts passed within the last thirty years municipal authorities are enabled under various conditions and restrictions to provide libraries and museums, markets, slaughter-houses, baths and work-houses, and even in some cases dwelling-houses for artisans and labourers. It is therefore on the whole clear that if it ever was a principle of English legislation that governing bodies are not to become makers or sellers of commodities, that principle must now be adopted with large reservations. Where profit can be made sufficient to tempt private capital to embark in the business, and where competition can be relied on to prevent the evils of monopoly, it is as true as ever that the public is best served by keeping the trade in private hands ; but where these conditions are not to be found, and where the matter is of such a kind that a public governing body can properly manage it, experience and analogy show that there is no *a priori* or absolute objection to the state, whether in the form of the central government or of a local authority, acting as a trader itself.

CHAPTER XI.

THE Post-Office is the great instance of a trading operation done by the government for the public, and the success it has achieved is constantly appealed to by those who advocate the assumption by government of other trading operations.

History.[1]—There appears to have been nothing in the nature of a public post till the reign of Charles I. In that reign posts from London to the north, the east, and the west, were established under the charge of a Postmaster-General, and a monopoly of carrying letters was claimed by the Crown. This claim was at first disputed, but was afterwards confirmed by the House of Commons; and the enterprise of the Common Council of London, who in 1649 set up a mail post in opposition to that of the government, was promptly suppressed. At first the Postmaster-General was allowed to make what profit he could after paying the expenses, the charges for letters being fixed; afterwards the office was farmed, and it was not till the end of the eighteenth century that the practice of farming came entirely to an end. In 1683

---

[1] For a summary of the history of the Post-Office, see the first report of the Postmaster-General presented to Parliament in 1855.

a penny post for London was established by one Robert
Murray, and assigned by him to one William Dockwra.
It met with some success, and was seized by the
government as an infringement of their monopoly.　In
the hands of the government it became the well-known
twopenny post, which existed as a separate department
of the Post-Office until 1854.　The net revenue arising
from the profits of the Post-Office, which in 1663 had
been conferred on the Duke of York, was in 1685 settled
on the King; and was then estimated to amount to
£65,000 a year.　In 1720 the cross posts of the country
were farmed to one Ralph Allen of Bath, the original of
Fielding's Squire Allworthy, who much improved them,
and made a large fortune by the undertaking.　In 1784
a further improvement was effected by sending the
letters in well appointed mail coaches, instead of by the
miscellaneous and untrustworthy messengers to whom
they had been previously intrusted.　This improvement
was due to the suggestion of Mr. Palmer of Bath, and
to the sagacity of Mr. Pitt, who overruled the opposition
of the Post-Office.　To Mr. Palmer was committed the
carrying out of his plan, which he did with great ability
and with much success, so far as concerned the public in
terest.　As regarded himself the success was not so great,
for he seems to have been deprived by the government
of a large part of the consideration which they had pro-
mised him.　Various other improvements, including the
carriage of the mails by railway, were from time to time
made by the Post-Office authorities, and in 1840 the
greatest improvement of all, viz. the uniform "Penny
Postage," was adopted on the suggestion of Sir Rowland
Hill.　The later history of the Post-Office is one of constant improvement, extension, and assumption of new

functions. The railway, the steamship, and the telegraph have come in aid of its operations, and it has not been slow to avail itself of these powerful auxiliaries. Its ubiquitous machinery has lent itself easily to simple money dealings, and it has thus been able to supplement the banks of the wealthy by acting as banker for the poor. The following is a brief outline of its present functions.

Carriage of Letters.—The details of this service will be found in the *Postal Guide* and in the reports of the Postmaster-General. Here it will be sufficient to refer to the reduction of charge; the extension of Post-Offices; the increase in collections and deliveries; the establishment of pillar posts; the establishment of letter-boxes in the postal vans on railways; the assimilation of postage and receipt stamps; the registration of letters; the institution of and improvements in postcards; the newspaper and book post; and the international postal union, which extends many of these benefits to communication with the rest of the world; as illustration of the continued activity of the department.

As an indication of the growth of this part of the business, it may be mentioned that in 1839, before the establishment of the penny post, the number of letters sent per head of the population was 3; in 1840, just after its introduction, 7; in 1872 it had become 28; and in 1882 it was 35.[1] The actual number of letters sent was, in 1850, 347,069,071, or 13 per head of population; in 1860, 560,002,000, or 19 per head; in 1870, 847,000,000, or 27 per head; in 1880, 1,176,423,600, or 34 per head; besides which in 1880 there were 122,884,000 postcards.

[1] See 28th Report of Postmaster-General (c. 3324, p. 1.)

The following figures from the postal statistics of foreign countries show that the people of England avail themselves of the public post more than twice as much as do the people of the most forward of foreign countries :—

Letters sent.		Number per head of population.
United Kingdom	1,176,423,600	34
France	524,380,300	14
Germany	731,755,000	16
Holland	54,732,000	13
United States	878,468,700	17

Parcels Post.—This is a great development of the carrying functions of the Post-Office, and is important, not only on account of the immediate facilities which it will afford the public, but because it brings the postal system into much closer communication and harmony with the railway system of the country. The details of the plan are not yet in a sufficiently forward state to be made public, but it is obvious that they must render necessary a very large development both of carriage for the Post-Office by railway, and also of the subsidiary means of collection and distribution which the Post-Office now employs. The nearest railway station must become far more than ever the postal centre of the district, and the collection and delivery of 7lb. parcels will overtask the powers of walking postmen.

The sanction of parliament was given to this new development by the Act 45 and 46 Vict. ch. 74, and the chief features of the scheme which it sanctions are as follows :—

The rates of postage and weights of parcels are to be

For an Inland Parcel of a weight	Rate of postage.
Not exceeding 1lb.	3*d*.
Exceeding 1lb. and not exceeding 3lbs.	6*d*.
Exceeding 3lbs. and not exceeding 5lbs.	9*d*.
Exceeding 5lbs. and not exceeding 7lbs.	1*s*.

Power is reserved to make from time to time any alteration in these rates which the interest of the public may require.

The Post-Office is to collect the parcels and to deliver them at the railway-station, and has power to send an officer in charge of them. The railway companies are to receive the parcels and to carry them by any train by which parcels are conveyed, and to provide means for sorting them in the train. The Postmaster-General is to hand over to the railway companies $\frac{11}{20}$ths of his gross receipts from parcels, and this is to be paid to the Railway Clearing House and distributed by them amongst the railway companies in proportion to the receipts of the companies for parcel traffic. Provision is made for revision of the terms fixed by the act, and for referring disputes to arbitration.

Not only is no monopoly conferred on the Post-Office; but the rights of the companies to carry parcels on their own account is expressly reserved. The first effect of the proposed arrangement has consequently been that some of the railway companies have themselves reduced their own charges for carrying parcels.

As soon as the Inland Parcels Post is established, it will be worked in connection with the International Parcels Post which is now in operation. This will enable parcels to be posted from any part of the United Kingdom to every other country in Europe except Russia, and to Egypt and Asiatic Turkey.

Telegraphs.—These were first established by private companies, and the government bought them up in 1870. The capital of the debt incurred for this purpose amounts to £10,880,571, and the interest upon it to £326,417.

There can be no doubt that the price thus paid was a heavy one. There have also been heavy charges for improvements and extensions of the service,[1] but the telegrams sent have increased from 9,850,177, or ·3 per head of the population in 1870, to 31,345,861, or ·9 per head in 1881; and the income, £1,630,000, is now equal to the expenditure, £1,366,000, with the addition of the interest on the debt incurred for purchase. The number of private messages is about three for each four persons in the United Kingdom, and the proportion of telegrams to letters is as 1 to 44. In France the proportion of telegrams to letters is as 1 to 29; in Belgium 1 to 24; in Holland 1 to 22; and in Switzerland 1 to 23. But the proportion of telegrams to population is greater in England than in any of these countries except Switzerland.

[1] See 28th Report of the Postmaster-General, and Parliamentary Papers 47 and 64 of 1882.

Telephones.[1]—It has been decided upon appeal to the courts of law, that the Post-Office has the legal monopoly of this comparatively new means of communication, as well as of the Telegraphs. The Postmaster-General, however, has not thought it right to avail himself of this monopoly, either in order to exclude private enterprise, or to confer a monopoly on any one private agency. He has established, or is prepared to establish, telephonic communication by the Post-Office where it is found expedient to do so, whether there are already private agencies at work or not, and he has granted licenses, or is prepared to grant licenses, to private agencies, under conditions which may be regarded as giving adequate protection to the public and the department, without regard to the question whether telephonic communication is already established or not. In effect it would seem, from the action thus taken by the Postmaster-General, that there is to be no monopoly, at any rate until competition has been tried and it has been ascertained by experience what is the best mode of doing the business.

Post-Office Savings Banks.[1]—The Post-Office, having at every Post-Office throughout the country a local agency through which money can be received and paid, has undertaken the duty of banker for the poor. This part of its business commenced in 1861, and it has since rapidly increased. The number of accounts open was in 1865, 611,384, and the aggregate amount of capital £6,526,400; in 1870 the number of accounts was 1,183,153, and the capital £15,099,104; in 1875 the number of accounts was 1,777,103, and

---

[1] See 28th Report of Postmaster-General.

the capital £25,187,345; and in 1881 the number of accounts was 2,607,612, and the capital £36,194,495. The Post-Office also invests for depositors in Government Stock, and the aggregate amount which had been so invested was, in 1881, £875,086.

The operation of the Savings Banks has been facilitated since 1880 by the penny stamp savings scheme, enabling persons to invest in the Bank by placing twelve penny stamps on a given form and handing it in to any Post-Office as a deposit for a shilling. An average of about £250 a day has been received by this means, and the effect is seen in the reduction of the average amount of deposit from £2 14s. 5d. in 1880 to £2 in 1881, whilst the aggregate amount received has increased by more than a million.

Money Orders and Postal Orders.—The Post-Office also acts as a remitter of small sums of money. Money Orders are directions given by a postmaster at one place to a postmaster at another place to pay any sum of money not exceeding £10 to a particular person. Postal Orders are general orders for the payment to any person to be named in the order of certain given sums ranging from 1/- to 20/-, and they can be cashed at any Post-Office. Money Orders have been in force since 1850; Postal Orders only since 1880. The Money Order system has been extended to the colonies and to most foreign countries. The Inland Money Orders were, in 1881, 14,880,821 in number, and £23,848,936 in amount, showing a decrease of upwards of a million and a half in number and nearly a million in amount as compared with 1880. But on the other hand the Postal Orders were 4,462,920 in number, and £2,006,917 in amount; thus showing that they have to a considerable extent taken the place of Money Orders.[1]

Insurance and Annuities.—The Post-Office also offers facilities for insuring lives to a small amount, either by the payment of a lump sum or of an annual premium; and for the purchase of immediate or of deferred life annuities. But this part of the business has not hitherto proved a success. An endeavour is being now made to extend it by connecting it with the Savings Bank.

Revenue and Expenditure.—The gross revenue of the Post-Office in 1881 was £9,028,374, and the expenditure £5,927,899, showing a surplus of income of £3,100,475, from which, however, has to be deducted £326,417 as interest on the debt incurred for the purchase of telegraphs.

One interesting feature connected with the Post-Office is the successful employment of women in the office work. They now amount to 2,299, and the Postmaster-General states that their employment has been attended with so much advantage to the department that he proposes to add to the number.

General Observations.—There can be no doubt that the Post-Office is a striking instance of the way in which a service which is essentially a trading service can be performed by a department of the state. The Postmaster-General is a carrier, a transmitter of messages, a banker, and an investment broker. These functions his office discharges with more than average success, and with zealous attention to the growing wants of the nation.

But as this instance is often urged as one which justifies far more extended operations on the part of

[1] See 28th Report of Postmaster-General.

the state, such as the purchase and working of railways, it may be worth while to point out two or three special conditions and limitations which make the Post-Office service peculiar.

In the first place, the Post-Office has filled vacant gaps in business which private traders have not been willing or able to occupy. The carriage of letters was imperfectly performed, or not at all, when the Post-Office took it up; and when it had been taken up by them, the first great improvements originated with persons outside of the office. The investment and remittance of very small sums of money was a business which private bankers did not find it worth while to undertake. The ubiquitous organisation of the Post-Office has rendered these operations possible and even profitable in its hands, while it was impossible or unprofitable when attempted partially or on a smaller scale.

In the second place, the Post-Office have not undertaken a business which requires either manufacture, or invention and speculation. It has made use of existing and well-known agencies, where the only difficulty was one of organisation; where there were no great experiments to be made; where there was no risk of great losses; and no hope of extraordinary gains. It is a merit of the undertaking, regarded as an official institution, that there is very little of that speculative element in it which is the life-blood of commercial activity. In the one case under the Post-Office where the undertaking is as yet experimental and speculative, viz. that of telephones, the Postmaster-General has come to the conclusion that it is not wise to exclude private enterprise.

Finally, the service, excellent as it is, has not avoided

one peril, which makes cautious statesmen unwilling to
-extend their industrial functions, viz. the difficulty of
dealing with a large class of servants. No one who
has watched the pressure which the services can bring
to bear on government through the medium of members
of Parliament, will undervalue this danger.

CHAPTER XII.

THIS subject alone, if fully treated, would fill my whole space, and all I can do is to glance at a few salient points.

Growth of Railways.—The development of railway communication in Great Britain has been such as no government management, however good, could possibly have produced. The number of lines, the number and speed of trains, and the general comfort and convenience of our railway system, are greater than can be found in any other country. The number of miles of railway open was 10,433 in 1860, and 18,175 in 1881. The tonnage of goods carried was 90,000,000 in 1860 and nearly 250,000,000 in 1881. The number of passengers carried, exclusive of season ticket holders, was 163,000,000 in 1860, and 626,030,000 in 1881. What is still more important as evidence of the service which the railways are rendering to the mass of the people, is that third-class passengers have increased from about 94,000,000 in 1860 to 523,000,000 in 1881. The capital, which was about £350,000,000 in 1860, was £745,500,000 in 1881, and the dividends had slightly increased. The danger rate, as shown by the proportion of casualties to the amount of travelling, has sensibly diminished.   What is still more important is, that the whole of this has been done by private capital and enterprise, unaided by government direction or by any grant of public money.   The only thing which the legislature has given to the companies is the power to take land, and for this they have had to pay, directly or indirectly, an enormous price.   On the other hand, they still remain subject to a passenger duty from which all other forms of locomotive enterprise are now free.

Legislation.—There has been constant legislation on the subject of railway traffic.   Eight committees and commissioners have made long and elaborate reports, and there have been about forty general acts, besides the special acts of the different companies.   The legislature has provided an elaborate code of laws for the protection of landowners, of road trustees, and of gas and water companies; and there are many enactments having the safety of passengers for their object, to which further reference will be made below.   There have also been provisions of the most elaborate kind fixing the capital of the railway companies, their borrowing powers, and the financial arrangements of the shareholders *inter se*— matters which really concern themselves, and not the public.   These matters, according to the principles of recent legislation concerning other joint-stock companies, are left to the partners themselves, and to the operation of the ordinary law of debtor and creditor, from which railway companies have been excluded.

As regards the commercial business of the railways, and the protection of the public from monopoly, the principal provisions are as follows :—

Limitation of Rates and Fares.—The charges on all railways are limited by their special acts. This limitation is in most cases inoperative, since the maximum rates fixed by the acts are in general considerably higher than the rates which the company find it their interest to charge. Indeed, it is obvious that, without power to revise the tolls periodically according to the altered circumstances of a railway, any attempt to fix them once for all by anticipation must be nugatory. As population, capital, trade, and manufacture increase, traffic increases also, and a charge which would have been moderate if levied on the small traffic which existed when the railway was made becomes exorbitant when multiplied by the increase of traffic. The interest of the companies in developing traffic, although it may under certain circumstances be an insufficient safeguard, is yet a better safeguard than any standard of tolls and charges fixed at the time when the company commences operations. Still, the parliamentary limit, which can always be revised when a company seeks fresh powers from Parliament, is an important security against possible extortion.

Limitation of Profits.—In some of the earlier private bills, Parliament adopted its favourite notion of limiting the profits of the company to a 10 per cent. dividend. And in 1844 an act [1] was passed enabling the Treasury, in the case of any railway constructed after the 1st of January 1845, upon the expiration of twenty-one years from the passing of its private act, and in the event of its profits for three years exceeding 10 per cent., to revise the tolls. The Treasury were in like manner, after twenty-one years, enabled to purchase the railway. But

[1] 7 & 8 Vict. ch. 85.

the power of revision of tolls was to be accompanied by a guarantee from the state of a constant 10 per cent. dividend ; and the purchase was only to be effected at the rate of twenty-five years' purchase of the actual annual profits, or, if they should be less than 10 per cent., at an additional price to be fixed by arbitration ; and neither revision nor purchase were to be effected without a special Act of Parliament.

How ineffectual any such limitation of profits would be, if exercised, we shall see in the case of gas companies. In the case of railway companies, a 10 per cent. dividend is seldom, if ever, made.

Government Purchase.—As regards the power of purchase, the conditions attached to it, viz. that the power should only apply to companies entirely made after 1844, that the price should be determined as above mentioned, and that the purchase should only be effected by a special Act of Parliament, reduce the power to little more than an unnecessary notice to the companies that the government might at some future time bring before Parliament a scheme for the purchase of railways. Nay, the companies actually procured in one of the recitals of the act in question a recognition of the very questionable principle that it was not the meaning of Parliament that companies should be exposed to competition with railways owned or conducted by government.

Cheap Trains.—Provisions were also made by Parliament [1] requiring companies to carry poor persons at what were then considered cheap rates, giving to the companies in return exemption in respect of these trains from passenger duty. Here, again, the impossibility of determining charges beforehand is well illustrated. It

[1] 1 & 2 Vict. ch. 98 ; 7 & 8 Vict. ch. 85.

has become the most profitable part of the business of many companies to carry third-class passengers at less than the parliamentary cheap fares; and the only result of the enactment is an exemption from general taxation, a constant dispute between the companies and the Chancellor of the Exchequer, and an inducement to the companies to disarrange their natural and beneficial traffic in order to get the benefit of the exemption.

Carriage of Mails.—It was not thought expedient [1] in making the concessions to the companies, to require from them in return any service in carrying the mails. The Post-Office can require them to carry mails and mail-guards, but for all such service it has to pay just as any private person would do. In the present state of things, in rural districts, where the station has superseded the old village and is the centre of communication for the country side, it is often desirable that the post-office as well as the telegraph should be there concentrated, and it seems desirable that the guards of all or any trains should take charge of and deliver letter-bags, as they do small parcels. However this may be, it is one of the merits of the new parcel-post that it will bring the railways and the post-office into closer connection.

Forwarding Traffic.—As regards intercommunication between different railways and joint arrangements for continuous traffic, the legislature in 1854 [2] did provide that the companies should afford reasonable facilities for forwarding each other's traffic, but it rendered the enactment nugatory by placing the power of enforcing it in the hands of an ordinary court of justice.

[1] 1 & 2 Vict. c. 98. 7 & 8 Vict. c. 85.
[2] 17 & 18 Vict. c. 31.

I

Joint Committee of 1872.—The subsequent history and results of legislation concerning railway companies, considered in their commercial aspect, are fully given in the Report of the Joint Committee of the Lords and Commons on Railway Amalgamation in 1872.[1] Their conclusions are, in general terms, that the efforts of Parliament to prevent amalgamation and secure competition had failed; that there is real and effective competition, especially in the carriage of heavy goods, through the medium of sea traffic; that competition by canal cannot be relied on; that there is real competition between railways themselves in the matter of facilities, but little in the matter of charges; that where competition does not regulate charges the self-interest of the companies leads them to develop new and promising traffic, and to promote competition between distant seats of trade or manufacture by neutralising distances; and that although in so doing they may be exposed to the charge of making some parts of their system pay for others, their action is probably advantageous to the public as well as themselves; that self-interest does not always lead them to make the lowest profitable charges, or to maintain water communications which are in their control, or to forward traffic by the shortest and best route, or to make or promote new lines; and the general recommendations of the Committee are as follows :—

" 1. Effectual competition by sea exists, and ought to be guarded by preventing railway companies from obtaining control over public harbours.
" 2. Competition by river and canal exists to a partial and limited extent only, and many important links of canal navigation are in the hands of railway

[1] Rl. Parl. Paper 364, 1872.

companies whose interest it often is to depreciate them. It is important that an effort should be made to maintain the competition which now exists, and it is still more important, whether competition is maintained or not, that the capacities of inland navigation should be fully utilised and developed.

"3. Equal mileage rates are inexpedient.

"4. It is impracticable to establish any standard for the revision of rates and fares founded on cost and profit.

"5. There would be much difficulty, and little, if any, gain to the public in determining a maximum scale of 'terminal charges.'

"6. Immediate reduction of rates and fares, even when practicable, cannot be looked upon as permanently effectual.

"7. Periodical revision of rates and fares is impracticable without some standard of revision.

"8. Revision of rates and fares founded on a limitation of dividend to a fixed amount is undesirable in the interest of the public.

"9. Revision of rates and fares founded on a division of profit above a certain amount between the companies and the public in this country is attended with great, if not insuperable, difficulties.

"10. A new and uniform classification of rates is desirable and practicable, and there should be power to alter the classification from time to time with consent of the commissioners mentioned below.

"11. The companies ought to be compelled by exhibition of their books at every station to inform the public what rates they charge for goods to all stations to which they book, distinguishing between mileage and 'terminals,' and giving all special rates and contracts. If complaint is made that this condition is not properly complied with, the commissioners mentioned below should have power to enforce it.

"12. If a *primâ facie* case is made raising a suspicion that any company is charging unequally or unfairly, contrary to the principles of the Railway and Canal Traffic Act, the commissioners should have power to call upon the company to state their reasons for such charges.

" 13. There is serious difficulty in any general legislation on the subject of workmen's trains, but where they are proved to be needed, the obligation to run them may properly be imposed as a condition of amalgamation.

" 14. Whilst on the one hand there may be amalgamations so large as to be objectionable, and whilst on the other there are cases in which amalgamation is obviously desirable, it is impossible to rearrange the railway map, or to determine by any general scheme what amalgamations shall be allowed, and what shall not.

" 15. In the event of branch railways being wanted and being refused by the existing companies, power should be given to local authorities to make them, or to guarantee the existing companies a moderate return on the necessary capital; and on such guarantee being given, the companies should be bound to make and work the line. If differences should arise between the local authorites and the companies, they should be settled by the said commissioners.

" 16. The Railway and Canal Traffic Act ought to be explained by enabling every railway company to make through rates and fares from or to any station on its own line, to or from any station on any other line, the rates to be divided as a general rule according to mileage after allowing for terminals; but with a provision that if any objection be made to the proposed rate or division as unfair, and no agreement can be come to, the commissioners mentioned below shall, upon the application of any of the companies interested, decide the matters in dispute.

" 17. Running powers may usefully be given in certain cases, and the propriety of giving them should be carefully considered by the joint committee hereafter

mentioned.   But it is not practicable or desirable to
give to railway companies generally running powers
over the lines of other companies, or to treat these
powers as conditions to be imposed by general legislation.   Differences as to running powers when given
should be settled by the said commissioners.

"18. The administration of the Railway and Canal
Traffic Act ought to be assigned to a special tribunal,
possessing knowledge of railway management.   Such
a tribunal will be found in the railway commission
mentioned below.

    *   *   *   *   *   *

"21. To perform the various duties referred to in this
report, a special body should be constituted, entitled
the Railway and Canal Commission, which should
consist of not less than three members.   They should
be persons of high standing, of whom one should
be an eminent lawyer, and one should be thoroughly
acquainted with the details and practice of railway
management."

These recommendations were acted on by the passing
of the Regulation of Railways Act 1873, (36 & 37 Vic.
c. 48) and the appointment of commissioners under it
with the powers recommended by the joint committee.
The number of cases under it has not been large, and
its decisions have often been defeated by appeal to the
law courts in the form of a writ of prohibition.   But
there can be no doubt that the tendency of public opinion
is in favour of strengthening the hands of the commission,
and the report of the recent Committee of the House of
Commons in 1881 and 1882 makes explicit suggestions
for that purpose.   Upon other points the opinion of
that committee was much divided, and it would be
premature to attempt to say what the result is likely
to be.   One question which occupies a large part of

the discussions before the committee concerns the inequality of rates. When this inequality arises from caprice, or negligence, or partiality, it is clear that there ought to be a summary and stringent remedy. But when it arises from a desire on the part of the companies to meet competition, or to develop a growing traffic which would not otherwise exist, where, in short, it is due to the ordinary trading motives, it would be contrary to authority, to analogy, and to the best interests of the public, to put an end to it. To say to the companies that they shall not reduce their rates in favour of one customer unless they reduce them in favour of all, is to put an end to that competition and that desire of profit which is a far more effectual security for moderate rates than any legislative restriction of charges can possibly be.

Competition.—It is probable that the competition which really exists, especially for goods traffic, has been somewhat underrated. Living in an island, as we do, with seaports on every coast, there exists a virtual competition not only between the places which are themselves upon the sea, but also between all places which are accessible from the sea by different lines of rail. There is an intense competition for traffic to the midland counties between London, Liverpool, Hull, and other seaports, and the several railways which lead from them. There is a further form of competition, in the possibility of new lines ; and such cases as the Hull and Barnsley Railway, recently authorised by Parliament, show that this form of competition has not entirely lost its power. These different forms of competition have been treated in a recent official report on the French railway system prepared by M. Waddington, as reasons why French railway companies, which are not exposed to competition, give the public fewer advantages than English railways, and require a different treatment. It is to be hoped that we shall not sacrifice this advantage to any dreams of equalization of railway rates, dreams which when investigated are generally found to originate in the very natural and common but not the less mischievous desire for protection from trade competition.

CHAPTER XIII.

MERCHANT shipping has already been mentioned as one of the greatest of our trading interests. Its enormous magnitude, its special importance to the nation, and the peculiarity of its character and circumstances, justify a separate chapter, for the purpose of showing how constant, how intimate, and how peculiar are the relations of the State to a merchant ship from the day when she becomes a ship to the day when she is broken up or abandoned. Under these relations are comprised, as stated above, not only the direct action of the executive, but the special laws and customs which govern this form of mercantile property.

Measurement and Registry.—When a ship is first built she is measured by a Government officer for her official tonnage. This measurement answers various purposes. It is the standard by which the ship is taxed for light, harbour, and dock dues. It denotes the size of the hull and its capacity for carrying cargo. Taken in connection with other particulars, it determines the identity of the ship. The present mode of measurement, which was due chiefly to the late Mr. Moorsom, and which is embodied in the Merchant Shipping Act of 1854, is founded on the principle of ascertaining the exact cubical capacity of the ship, and giving the results in tons, each of which contains 100 cubic feet.

It has given general satisfaction, and has been adopted by all foreign nations.   But certain anomalies, arising out of questionable exemptions, originally introduced to meet the claims of particular interests, as well as out of new methods of construction, have arisen in the English law ; and with the view of removing these anomalies a Royal Commission was recently appointed. The majority of this commission recorded their strong approval of the principle of the existing law, and made certain recommendations, which, if adopted, would have the effect of removing the existing anomalies, and of bringing English law into harmony with that of other nations.   A small minority recommended the abandonment of the present principle of ascertaining the cubical contents of the hull, and the substitution of a principle long since discarded, viz., that of displacement.   Any such change is really out of the question, both because it is not an improvement in itself on the present method, and because it is contrary to the practice of the world. But the action of the minority of the committee has had the effect of making the removal of defects in the existing law more difficult than it would otherwise be.

When the ship is measured, her name is entered in an official register book, kept at each port by the officers of customs, with a full description, and the name of the owner.   An official copy of the entry on parchment, called the Certificate of Registry, is given to the owner of the ship, and always afterwards goes with her till she is broken up, or otherwise ceases to be a British ship. It is this document which identifies her and gives her the right to carry the British flag. The name which is inscribed on it cannot be altered without official sanction. For the purpose of further identifying her and preventing the confusion which would arise from a number of ships with the same name, an official number is given her, which is entered in the register book and certificate of registry, and is also permanently marked on the ship herself. Her name, port of registry, and draft of water, are also marked under official inspection on the outside of the ship.

The register of the ship kept in the book at the Custom House constitutes the title to the ship. The name and address of each owner, with the number of shares belonging to him, is entered upon it, and any transfer or mortgage of the ship or shares is entered in the same book, whenever and wherever it occurs. No notice is taken of any trusts, and any innocent purchaser who takes a conveyance from the persons whose names are on the register has an absolute and indefeasible title. A copy of every entry made on the register at any port is sent every day to the Registrar General of shipping in London, who is an officer of the Board of Trade; and there is thus in his books a complete and trustworthy record of the actual title of every British ship; and this record can be consulted on the payment of a trifling fee. In this way the State provides for the owners of merchant ships a complete system of title and conveyance, so that the transfer of a vessel worth £100,000 may be completed for a shilling.

The title of any British ship may be transferred from any port in the British Empire to any other, by a simple letter between the registrars at the two ports, which is sent on application by the registered owner; and if an owner wishes to deal with his ship at a distance from her port of registry, he can get from the registrar an ambulatory form of registry which enables him to make a complete title to a distant purchaser.

When the ship is broken up, lost, or sold to a foreigner, a report has to be made to the registrar; the certificate of registry is given up to him, and the register is closed.

Officers and Crew.—The officers of a merchant ship are required to pass examinations in technical proficiency, and to produce evidence of character; they then receive certificates enabling them to act as masters, mates, and engineers.

The crews of ships which are employed on voyages beyond the river Elbe and Brest, are engaged in a public office before a public officer, and the terms of the engagement are read out and explained to the seamen. Elaborate provisions are made by the Merchant Shipping Acts for preventing desertion and maintaining discipline; but in these, considerable alterations have recently been made. Desertion, and refusal to join after engagement, were formerly treated as criminal offences, and are still so treated by the laws of most nations. But, following the principles which have been adopted in the law governing other contracts of employment, Parliament has recently repealed the enactments which gave these criminal remedies; and refusal to perform a contract to serve at sea is now treated like other refusals to serve, as a breach of civil contract. The penalties for breaches of discipline by a seaman when he has joined his ship are retained intact. It cannot be denied that this change in a long-established

practice has been productive of some temporary inconvenience, and that desertions have increased within the
last two years. But it is to be hoped and expected
that this inconvenience will be but temporary; that the
ultimate effect of the change will be to produce a better
and more wholesome relation between owners and their
crews; that the vicious practice of giving unnecessary
advances of wages may come to an end; and that in
lieu of this practice, with its demoralising temptations,
and the arbitrary powers of imprisonment, on which
shipowners have hitherto been led to rely for the
manning of their ships, there may be substituted those
inducements to voluntary service which are found
effectual in other branches of employment.

When the ship has gone to sea the law still follows
the crew; certain rights and duties are prescribed;
provision is made for enforcing them by means of the
consular staff and of the special naval courts, which
can be summoned for the purpose in foreign ports. No
men can be discharged abroad without provision for
their restoration to their own country; and when the
ship finally returns home to this country, the crew are
discharged before a public officer, who sees that the men
are duly paid their wages, and settles disputes. He also
forwards money for the men to their wives and families,
and in many of the larger ports sees that seamen who
belong to some distant place are provided with immediate means of escaping from local temptations and
returning to their homes.

For such seamen as choose to invest their earnings, a
Seamen's Savings Bank is provided, into which men can
pay, and from which they can draw at every port in the
United Kingdom, in the same manner as from the Post-

Office Savings Banks, of which Seamen's Savings Banks were the forerunner.

Safety.—For this purpose also the State follows the ship throughout her active employment. Passenger steamers and ships carrying large numbers of emigrants must be inspected by officers of the Board of Trade, and must be reported to be safe ; and in the case of emigrant ships they must also be reported to be properly fitted, equipped, victualled, and manned.

The number of passengers is limited by the Board of Trade.

For the purpose of avoiding collision, all ships are required to carry certain lights, which are inspected by officers of the Board of Trade.

For the same purpose all ships are required, when they meet one another at sea, to obey certain rules ; and these rules are matters not only of municipal but of international obligation.

All ships are also required to carry a certain number of boats.

Passenger steamships are required to have properly adjusted compasses.

Special provisions are made with respect to grain cargoes and deck cargoes of wood.

Unsafe ships may be detained by the Board of Trade and its officers, subject to an appeal to a court of survey, and subject also to an action for damages, if in the opinion of a jury the detention has been wrong or improper.

The subject of unsafe ships has attracted much attention lately. The losses of life at sea are no doubt great, and much to be deplored ; nor should any effort be spared which can make them less. There are some

bad ships: there are many overladen ships: and, chief
cause of loss, there is recklessness and overhaste in navi-
gating ships.   Nor are the relations of our seamen to
their employers, or their own condition when thrown
ashore amid the temptations of our sea ports, what we
could wish them to be.   But to allege that shipowners
as a rule are worse than other people, or that ships
are worse and more unsafe than they formerly were,
is a gross and unjust exaggeration.   Our shipowners
have not made themselves masters of the carrying
trade of the world by building and sailing bad and
unsafe ships; and the loss of life at sea, so far as
can be ascertained, is, in proportion to our merchant
navy and its work, not greater but less than it was
in former years.

The operation of the measures which have recently
been adopted by Parliament in order to secure further
safety is extremely interesting.   One of these remedies
is administrative, viz. the power given to the Board of
Trade to detain unseaworthy ships, a power which,
since the Plimsoll agitation, has been exercised through
the means of a large staff of local surveyors in most of
the ports of the United Kingdom.   Another remedy is
judicial, viz. liability to criminal prosecution for sending an unseaworthy ship to sea.   The latter of these
remedies has always been difficult, because with all the
intermediate agencies which modern trade requires, it is
seldom easy to bring home culpability or negligence to
the owner, whose greed may notwithstanding have been
the real cause of the unseaworthiness.   But the criminal
remedy has been rendered absolutely ineffectual by the
administrative remedy.   When a shipowner has been
prosecuted for sending a ship to sea in a grossly

unseaworthy condition, and the fact has been distinctly proved, the answer has been that the Board of Trade might have stopped the ship, and did not do so; as if the Board of Trade and its officers were ubiquitous and omnipresent. But however this may be, the answer has been and will be accepted by judge and jury as conclusive in answer to a criminal charge; and the criminal remedy for culpable unseaworthiness is therefore one which can seldom, if ever, be enforced. Nor is the working of the administrative remedy satisfactory. Many unsafe ships are actually detained, and more are indirectly deterred from going to sea. But the appeal for damages which is given from a responsible department to a judge and jury, who do not perhaps know the stem from the stern of a ship, is an appeal from Philip sober to Philip drunk, and tends to cripple administrative action. On the other hand, to subject the shipowner to detention without appeal would be to subject him to possible official tyranny and caprice. Again, the power of detention in isolated cases involves much more extensive interference. When a particular ship is detained, say, for overloading, the shipowner retorts with much justice, "Why do you stop me when on the point of going to sea? Why not tell me beforehand what you require?" And this the Board of Trade cannot do without laying down fixed rules both as to load line and as to other matters, which would place the whole mercantile marine in official fetters. Such are the difficulties of interference, and they are as yet unsolved.

One cause of unseaworthiness, the most important perhaps of all, is the law and practice of marine insurance. A policy of insurance is in theory a contract of

indemnity.   But the practice of the trade and the
decisions of the judges have made it much more. A ship
can be insured so that her loss shall be a certain gain
to the shipowner, and the courts of law will enforce
this liability against the underwriter.   I have seen a
letter from a shipowner regretting that a certain ship was
not lost ; and I have heard a shipowner complain that he
had been specially unlucky because an old ship of his
had been lost on her first voyage after he had sold her,
whereas if she had been lost whilst she belonged to him,
he would have realised enough from the insurance to
enable him to buy a good, new, modern ship !   In such
cases the shipowner may not purposely lose his ship,
but it is idle to suppose that he will take the same care
of her as if he were not insured, or insured only to a
moderate amount.   The evil is one which it is not easy
to cure.   It is very difficult to interfere with improper
contracts of insurance without interfering mischievously
with innocent and proper contracts. Further, it is not the
interest of any traders as a class to prevent over-insurance.
The underwriters, as a class, profit by it ; and though the
individual underwriter who has to pay for a loss suffers,
and is often not unwilling to contest a bad case, the
law, which countenances over-insurance, does not enable
him to resist payment unless he can prove actual fraud
to the satisfaction of a jury ; and this he can seldom do,
not only from the inherent difficulty of obtaining evidence, but because he comes into court in the character
of a man who, having made a bargain by which he turns
out to be a loser, is trying to escape from it.   In the
excitement caused by the Plimsoll agitation the Government did make an effort to amend the law of insurance.
A bill was introduced for this purpose at the beginning

of the session of 1876.   But other business intervened
and the bill was no more heard of.

Lighthouses, Harbours, and Pilots.—The State provides
these adjuncts to safe navigation, although the money by
which they are supported is raised by dues levied upon the
ships which use them.   General lights and seamarks are
managed by the Trinity House and by the Scotch and
Irish Lighthouse Boards, under a certain control by the
Board of Trade ; and local lights, harbours, and pilots
are managed by local bodies, generally representative in
character.

Wrecks and Casualties.—When a ship is lost on our
own coasts careful provision is made for the purpose of
rendering assistance and saving life, both by means of
life boats, which belong to and are managed by a
charitable association, and by means of the rocket
apparatus, which is worked by the coastguard and by
voluntary brigades under the direction of the Board of
Trade.   The coastguard also act as police in protecting
wrecked property, and the officers of customs acting as
receivers of wreck take charge of such property and
restore it to the owners.

Provision is also made for inquiries into the causes of
wrecks.   A preliminary inquiry is first made in all cases
by the officers of the Board of Trade ; and in more important cases a public investigation is subsequently held in
judicial form before the wreck commissioner or before
two justices, aided by professional assessors.   In cases
of culpable default by the masters or officers, these courts
have power to cancel or suspend their certificates.   The
reports of all these investigations are made public.

Maritime Law.—The executive government thus
follows a ship throughout her career, from her first

construction to her final destruction. But in addition to this constant intervention of the executive, the state supplies a code of special rules, in respect of collision, liability for damage, salvage, insurance, and bottomry, &c., not to mention maritime prize and capture, which constitute a large and special branch of the general law; which owe their existence to the necessities of shipping; and many of which have the peculiarity that they are international as well as municipal.

General Observations.—Under these circumstances it is interesting to see how large a part the state plays in respect of this great national interest. The motive power, the energy, the invention, the skill, the courage, to which it owes its success, are those of individual Englishmen. Nor are they in any way protected by the state from the most severe competition. But the state watches over, helps, fosters, restricts and regulates a British merchant vessel from the day when her materials assume the form of a ship to the day when they finally lose that form, both by official regulation and by a system of peculiar law. Whatever be the result of these different actions of the state, one thing is quite certain; viz. that the aggregate effect of all of them has not ·been to destroy the prosperity of this great interest, or to prevent a development unexampled in the history of the world. The shipping of the United Kingdom has increased from 3,397,000 tons of sailing ships and 168,000 tons of steamships in 1850 to 3,851,000 tons of sailing ships and 2,723,000 tons of steamships in 1880, and there is a considerable further increase in 1881. Taking one ton of steam tonnage to be equal to to four tons of sailing tonnage, the tonnage of the United Kingdom was 42 per cent. of the known oversea tonnage of all the maritime countries of the world in 1860, and 55 per cent. in 1880. No foreign country, least of all our former rival, the United States, comes any where near us. The current expenditure on our ships and the income we derive from them are enormous. The fixed capital employed in our shipping is probably about £110,000,000, but the annual outgoings on shipping, which constitute an invisible export, and which give employment to an immense amount of English labour, probably amount to more than one-half of that sum ; whilst the income from our shipping, which returns to us in the shape of imports, is not less than and probably more than £60,000,000 a year.[1] From these facts I should draw two conclusions ; first, that, this great interest has on the whole benefited and not suffered by the action of the state ; and, secondly, that, considering the magnitude of this interest, and its successful development, it is one of which the nation may well be proud, and in dealing with which hasty and ill-considered measures are much to be deprecated.

[1] See Mr. Giffen's paper on the use of import and export statistics in the *Journal of the Statistical Society*, for June, 1882.

CHAPTER XIV.

ACTION OF THE STATE WITH RESPECT TO FOREIGN TRADE ;
ABANDONMENT OF PROTECTION AND DISCRIMINATIVE
DUTIES.

AMONG the various actions of the state which are
intended to increase and foster trade, there is one form
of interference which in this country we have ceased to
practise, it is to be hoped, for ever ; I mean protection
of home against foreign industries. Whether in the
older form of prohibition, or in the newer form of
differential duties, we have abandoned the attempt to
promote our own industries by preventing our people
from buying the produce of the industries of other
nations. The subject is old and worn, but considering
the protectionist doctrines which still hold their ground
in other countries, and the recent attempt to revive
similar opinions in our own, it is worth while to state
once more as shortly as possible what are the
grounds of our present action, or rather inaction, in
this matter.

In the first place, as even protectionists admit, to
keep out anything which is made better and cheaper
abroad than at home, makes those of our own people

who want that article pay more for it and get less of it, or get it of worse quality, than they would do if allowed to buy the foreign article. To keep out American corn or French silk makes people in England who want corn or silk pay more for these articles and get them in less quantity and of worse quality. The importance of this to us, who import one-third of our food, and are every year importing more and more of it, and of whose total imports, amounting to more than £400,000,000, ninety per cent. are either food or materials for our manufactures, is obvious, and it might be sufficient to leave the matter here. We are not likely to starve our working population or to ruin our manufactures. But this is only a part of the evil of protection, and does not go to the root of the question.

Protection is intended for the benefit of producers at the expense of consumers; for the benefit, that is to say, of the landowner, at the expense of the rest of the people; for the benefit of the manufacturer at the expense of those who use what he makes; and it is alleged by the advocates of protection that in the benefit thus given to the landowner or manufacturer, and to the persons whom they employ, is found a compensation, and more than a compensation, for the mischief done to the consumer.

But this is not so. In the first place protection often— perhaps generally—injures the very persons it is meant to benefit. It makes them rely on the false support of an artificial law, instead of on their own brains and hands. The exclusion of competition deadens industry and skill. British shipping, for instance, never flourished when certain trades were reserved to it by our navigation laws, so much as it has done since every flag was admitted to compete with it in every branch of our trade.

But this may not always be the case. It is possible, we must admit, that a weak industry may be kept alive by excluding its foreign rivals. Englishwomen might give more custom to Coventry, if they could not buy the cheaper and better ribbons which are made at Lyons and Basle. The Coventry ribbon-makers might for a time make more profits and pay more wages. Assuming this to be the case, the effect, not only to the women who buy silk, but to the whole producing industry of the country, will nevertheless be mischievous ; for we can only pay for the French and Swiss ribbons by sending to France and Switzerland something which we make better and cheaper than the French or Swiss can make it ; so much better and cheaper, that it will bear the cost of carriage, and yet be preferred to the French or Swiss article. It may be iron, or cotton, or cloth ; and it may be that we do not send it to France or Switzerland, but to India or China, and that India or China in turn sends tea or indigo to France, and that what we make is so cheap and good that it bears all this cost of carriage, to the great benefit of our own shipowners. It is impossible to trace the complicated course of trade, but one thing is certain, viz., that we cannot buy the French or Swiss ribbons without making and selling something which we can make better and cheaper than ribbons, and which consequently brings more profit to our manufacturer, and better wages to our workmen. If we put a stop to the buying of French ribbons we also put a stop to this better industry of our own, in order to encourage the inferior industry of the Coventry ribbon-maker. Ribbons are a comparatively small industry, but what is true of them is true of all the larger elements of trade—of cotton, cloth, iron, and agricultural produce. We are all consumers, and we are all in some sense producers. Regarded as consumers it is admitted that protection is injurious to us; but what is not so generally recognised, is that protection is equally injurious to us considered as producers. It prevents us from doing what we can do best. It makes us produce what we produce badly and scantily, instead of what we can produce well and abundantly. It makes what we buy and use dearer and worse; but at the same time it also limits and reduces the business and profits of our producers, and the wages they pay to their workmen.

But this is not all. One protectionist step brings on another. Every product of industry is a means, the raw materials, so to speak, of other industries. In making it dear and scarce we cripple them ; and they, in their turn, must be protected. Keep out foreign paper, and foreign books must be kept out. Keep out foreign iron, and all that is made of iron—ships, machinery, tools—must be kept out too. Keep out tools and machinery, and all that tools and machinery produce must be kept out also. And thus the protectionists get into a vicious circle, in which everybody without exception is plundered or injured, and in which everybody plunders, except the particular producer, who has such natural advantages that he has no foreign rival. To him protection brings no benefit, whilst he is the victim of other protectionists. And yet, he is the one who if left to enjoy his natural advantages could and would do more than any other for himself and his country. Everything is made dear to all consumers ; and all

producers are restricted in production.   If any gain
by the plunder it is the few who gain at the expense of
the many; and the aggregate gain by plunder must be
very small as compared with the aggregate loss.   Dear
living is ill compensated by high wages; and what is
still worse for the whole of the productive classes, they
are prevented from making the most which nature
has enabled them to make out of their labour and
skill.

CHAPTER XV.

General Principles.—In most of the cases we have
been considering there is little, if any, doubt about the
principles which should guide the relations of the state
to trade. That the state should enforce within certain
limits the obligation of contracts; and that it should
determine weights and measures, and supply a standard
of value and medium of exchange; is admitted by all
civilised nations, and by all philosophers. That the
state should not create monopolies where they can be
avoided, and should carefully limit them, where inevitable, is also scarcely disputed. That the state should
trade itself only where private interest will not supply
what is needed, or where the evils of monopoly cannot
otherwise be remedied, is a general maxim, in this
country at any rate. And finally we shall, most of us,
agree in condemning all attempts to protect native
industry by prohibitions or differential duties.

But we now approach a class of cases in which it is
more difficult to find any leading principle. They are
cases in which the state specially interferes with,
regulates, and restricts the freedom of private dealings

in special trades which are not monopolies; sometimes for the purpose of seeing that the bargain is duly performed by the parties to the contract, or by one of them; but more often for the purpose of guarding some interest outside the original dealing, and the interests of the parties to it.

In dealing with this subject I find myself inevitably dealing with the same class of questions with which Mr. Stanley Jevons has dealt in his treatise on the *State in Relation to Labour;* and am disposed to agree with him when he says (p. 6) that "We must rid our minds of the idea that there are any such things in social matters as abstract rights, absolute principles, indefensible laws, unalterable rules, or anything whatever of an eternal and inflexible nature;" and that "The state is justified in passing any law, or even in doing any single act, which without ulterior consequences, adds to the sum total of happiness." "Not less true is it," he says (p. 14) that "The modern English citizen who lives under the burden of the revised edition of the statutes, not to speak of innumerable municipal, railroad, sanitary, and other bye-laws, is after all an infinitely freer as well as nobler creature than the savage, who is always under the despotism of physical want—far freer too than the poor Indian, who, though perhaps unacquainted with written law, is bound down by the most inflexible system of traditional usage and superstition," and that "it is impossible that we can have the constant multiplication of institutions and instruments of civilisation which evolution is producing, without a growing complication of relations, and a consequent growth of social regulations."   At the same time I am disposed to think that though there are no absolute rules by which such legislation as we are about to consider can be limited, there are certain general principles or tendencies, which in this country at any rate, afford some general notion of the direction in which we should steer and do not leave us wholly at the mercy of casual winds and waves.

Freedom the General Rule.—Imperfect as our experience is, it has suggested certain general conclusions in favour of a larger amount of freedom—freedom of thought, freedom of speech, and freedom of action, than have been thought consistent with the welfare of the community in earlier times. Though these conclusions become false and misleading, if stated in the form of an absolute and universal rule, they are, I think, sufficiently well founded to warrant a general presumption in their favour, and to throw the burden of proof on those who wish to restrict freedom. Every grown person of the average European type under a reasonably strong and good Government is likely to do better for himself in matters of gain and profit than the Government, or other persons are likely to do for him ; and consequently, in general, the best thing to do for him is to leave him free to use his mind, his body, and his property as he finds best for himself. This maxim, or something of the kind, seems to me to be the sound foundation of modern political economy, and has in that capacity won great triumphs for mankind. It leaves abundant room for state interference on the grounds of public policy, of morality, of health, of safety, of the welfare of others, and even, in extreme cases, of the welfare of the person with whose liberty it is proposed to interfere. But it has, or ought to have the effect of throwing the burden of proof on those who propose interference with liberty. A man ought to be free to use his mind, his body, and his goods as he pleases until it is shown that his freedom will be followed by ill consequences of more importance than the good of which he is deprived by the restriction. It may be worth while to follow this a little farther, and point out in some detail what are the consequences of restriction.

Consequences of Restriction.—In the first place, any restriction is almost sure to bring some bad consequences to the person restricted. They may be very serious consequences, or they may be very slight, and they may be quite outbalanced by other consequences; but in itself, to prevent a man from doing what his self-interest leads him to do, does him some injury in pocket or in person. These evils are generally of an obvious kind, and are generally, when interference is proposed, sufficiently brought to notice by the complaints of the interests affected.

But, in the next place, there are the unseen consequences of restriction, which, as Mr. Jevons well observes, are often of more importance than the seen consequences. We do not know what amount of positive mischief we may be doing by specific modes of interference. No one supposed when the present system of public-house licenses was established, in the interest, as it was believed, of public morality, that it would lead to the creation of a large vested interest which renders it very difficult to do what public morality now requires. No one supposed when the registration of bills of sale was enforced by law, that it would tend to the encouragement and protection of the class of dealings it was intended to discourage.

Still less do we know what amount of good we may be preventing, and this is the more important consideration of the two. It may sound like an extreme and absurd case, but it is nevertheless true and good as an illustration, that if some extreme views which have been recently promulgated concerning public safety had been held and enforced in the time of Columbus, he might never have been allowed to endanger his crews by embarking them in his frail vessels on the hazardous voyage which ended in the discovery of America. If the restrictions on joint-stock enterprise which were in favour with some of our older lawyers and economists had continued to prevail, we should not only have been deprived of the widespread and gigantic development of industrial undertakings which has taken place in the last half century, but we should have had no idea of what we had lost. No one can tell at this moment what would happen in the way of increased production and consequent comfort to mankind if all the protective systems of the world were at once abolished. Restriction of human freedom is often felt and seen to be a burden, but our ignorance of its ultimate consequences is a far stronger objection to it.

Again, a system of restrictive interference negatives responsibility. It is impossible at once to dictate to a man what he shall do and to hold him responsible for the consequences. If a man is compelled to build a ship, or a railway, or a house in a particular way, he cannot be made answerable civilly or criminally for any consequences which may arise from building it in that way, however dangerous and destructive it may prove to be. You may have the responsibility of the state or the responsibility of the private person, but you cannot have both. The adoption of the one forces you to abandon the other. No judge or jury will find a shipowner guilty of negligence, however flagrant, if his actions, however culpable, have, or even might have, passed the ordeal of Government supervision. No employer can be held liable for consequences arising from the misconduct of his servants if the state has compelled him to employ them. This is not a matter of mere speculation, but of practical experience, as is shown by the failure of repeated attempts to procure convictions for the crime of sending unseaworthy ships to sea.

Again, the gain of a regulation enforced by law is often more apparent than real. A certain uniformity of good results is produced, but it is generally a low average. It is what the worst men in the trade can be compelled to do, not what the best men would do if left to themselves. For the motives of self-interest, of gain, of character, and of individual liability, a general and compulsory rule is substituted. The worst men will be made better, but the best men will probably become worse, and will act down to the rule. There will be more uniformity, but the average will most likely be lower.

Again, the intervention of Government tends to make persons less careful in looking after their own interests. If I can rely on a Government brand, I am the less likely to take pains to see that the article I buy is what I really want. The tendency is clearly to make me less energetic, less cautious, less able to help myself. This is a most important consideration. A community of men who are accustomed to look for everything to Government is likely to be less productive, less strong, less noble, less able to help themselves in the struggle for existence, than one in which each individual feels the necessity of relying on himself.

There are plenty of other objections to different forms of interference, such as the risk of corruption amongst a host of inspectors and administrators, the check to invention, ingenuity, improvement, and so on. But I have indicated here only the great *a priori* objections to all restrictions on individual liberty. They are of course only *a priori* objections, and do not and ought not to prevail when it can be shown that there are still greater objections to absolute freedom. But they are in my judgment sufficient to justify us in withholding assent to the proposition that there is no place for general propositions, or that every act ought be judged separately. I think there is ample ground for the general proposition that when it is proposed to restrict individual liberty, it rests with those who make the proposal to show that there will result from the restriction some positive good, or some prevention of evil which more than counterbalances the good which would result from the free action which is to be restricted.

It is in this spirit, at any rate, that I shall speak of the interferences of the State with freedom of action, which we are about to consider.

There is one suggestion mentioned in Mr. Jevons's essay which, in connection with this branch of the subject, seems to me to be especially important. It is the suggestion drawn from his own very instructive article in the *Contemporary Review* for January, 1880, vol. xxxvii., pp. 177-192, in which he shows that in many cases it is possible for the legislator to resort to direct experiment, and when he suggests "that before passing any great act of Parliament which will involve the whole of an extensive trade or class in some irrevocable and costly change, we ought to try experiments, and thus obtain the most direct and pertinent evidence concerning the probable result." I believe this to be a most fruitful suggestion. Ignorance of the real effect of proposed measures is the greatest difficulty of the legislator. In matters so complicated and delicate, experience is often the only guide, and experience procured by an experiment upon a whole nation is too costly to be lightly risked. If it were acknowledged to be right and proper to try local and special experiments in legislation, not only would many foolish interventions be prevented, but many good rules and practices which now never get an opportunity of proving and establishing their merits, might be tried and brought into use.

CHAPTER XVI.

ONE form of the State interference with special trades has for its object to make it sure that purchasers get the particular article they want, in proper quantity, quality, or condition. The most extreme form of this interference, fortunately exceptional in this country, is one in which the State by general law, or local law, or custom, undertakes to test the character of an article of commerce, and to guarantee that it possesses certain qualities. The following are the principal cases of this interference, so far as I have been able to ascertain them.

Gun-Barrels.—Compulsory tests for gun-barrels are of very early date. They seem to have existed under a Royal Charter granted to the Mystery of gun-makers as far back as 1637, and have been continued by subsequent statutes. These statutes were consolidated and re-enacted in 1868 by the Act 31 & 32 Vict. ch. 113. Under this act all barrels of guns or small arms of any kind must be proved and stamped either at the London or the Birmingham proof-house, and are not allowed to be sold in this country or exported unless so proved and stamped. The proving is in the charge of bodies representing the trade, and fees are paid to cover the expenses.

L

From the absence of complaint it may be presumed that this system works satisfactorily to the trade. It is to be observed that it is founded upon the privileges of the now obsolete guild; and also that there is involved in it the important element of public safety, over and above any commercial advantage which the stamping may be supposed to give to the articles sold.

Chain Cables and Anchors Acts, 1864, 1871, and 1874; 27 & 28 Vict. ch. 27; 34 & 35 Vict. ch. 101; 37 & 38 Vict. ch. 51.—Under these modern acts certain public bodies, to which the Government have power to add others, are authorised to erect testing-machines, and these machines are inspected and licensed by the Board of Trade. All chains and anchors sold for the use of British ships must be tested at one of these machines according to a scale approved by Order in Council, and must be stamped accordingly, under a penalty on both buyer and seller. A contract for the sale of a chain cable implies a warranty that it has been so tested. In this case also there is involved the element of safety to human life, with the addition that the practice of marine insurance has a tendency to weaken the motives which would otherwise induce the shipowner to provide adequately against danger and loss by seeing to the goodness of his own anchors and cables.

Hall-marking of Gold and Silver Plate.[1]—Under a number of old and confused statutes certain gold and

---

[1] A full account of this practice will be found in the Reports of the Select Committees of 1878 and 1879. Parl. Papers 328 of 1878 and 191 of 1879. This Committee condemned the duty; a majority supported compulsory hall-marking, but a strong majority, including Mr. Goschen, Mr. Courtney, and Mr. Thomson Hankey, condemned it.

silver articles are required to be of a certain standard
quality, and to be tested and marked with a certain
stamp by certain bodies, the chief of which is the
Goldsmiths' Company. These statutes no doubt originated in the desire to keep the precious metals and all
articles made out of them of one standard quality, that
quality being the quality of the metal used in the
coinage. But in the case of gold there are now six
different standards, which have been adopted to meet
the requirements of trade; and most gold articles in
common use are also expressly exempted. A great
number of silver articles are also exempted, leaving
silver plate almost the only article still subject to
this antiquated law. The machinery is as imperfect as
the law. There is no security for the due application of
one uniform test by the different bodies charged with
the duty of hall-marking. There is also an anomalous
and mischievous duty on silver plate, maintained
through the medium of the hall-marking system. The
majority of the London trades are in favour of the
retention both of the duty and the compulsory hall-
mark, a circumstance which is consistent with the
allegation that the compulsory system they advocate
is protective in its character. On the other hand, the
assailants of the present law complain that the system
of hall-marking, coupled with the duty, not only operates
to the exclusion of foreign plate, but interferes with
manufacture at home, and impedes the importation of
foreign manufactured silver. The manufacture of silver
plate is on the decline in England, whilst in the United
States, where there is no hall-marking, and where the
makers trust to their own marks, it is rapidly
progressing.

Herring-brand.[1]—In Scotland a system exists under which officers of the Scotch Fishery Board examine and brand the casks of cured herrings of those dealers, but of those dealers only, who choose to have the brand applied, and thus certify to the quality of the fish contained in them. The expense is paid for by fees charged to the persons whose casks are branded. Complaints have been made by some curers that the operation of this system is to reduce the standard of goodness, and to injure the trade; and a select committee was appointed in 1881, who by a large majority came to the conclusion that the trade generally approved the system of branding; that the catch and sale of fish had increased under it; that although the operation was voluntary and accompanied by payment of a fee, three-fourths of the trade elected to submit to the brand; and that the smaller fishermen were in favour of it, because it enabled them to compete with the larger firms whose produce and brands would be well known in the market without any official guarantee. It is to be observed that the system is voluntary; that it has been long in operation; that the brand is well known on the Continent; and that the majority of the trade are strongly in its favour. Under these circumstances it is not to be wondered at that the select committee should refuse to disturb a system which was working so well, whatever may be thought of some of the arguments adduced in support of it.

Cork Butter Market.—In this important market a system of examination and branding prevails under which in practice—if not in law—producers of butter are prevented from selling it, unless it has been branded

[1] Report of Select Committee, Parl. Paper 393, 1881.

by an official inspector.   Of this system the Royal
Commissioners on Agriculture report as follows :—

"The way in which trade may be hampered and its
progress obstructed by the abuse of arrangements
originally designed for its promotion is strikingly illustrated by the history of the Cork Butter Market, which
will be found in the evidence submitted to your
majesty.

"Whatever the value of the Cork Butter Market in
former times to the farmers may have been, it has now
ceased to be an institution that can be favourably
spoken of. Owing to the greater facilities for the transit
of produce there is a much larger demand for fresh
butter than formerly, and a corresponding diminution
in the value of very salt butter.

"The present arrangements of the Cork Butter
Market evidently tend to reduce the value of the
highest class of butter, and to unduly raise that of a
lower class, so as to produce an approximate uniformity
in price, which is not good either for the farmer or for
the consumer.

"The Cork Butter Market is in no real sense an
open market; on the contrary, the control of the
Corporation of Cork over it is illusory, and the management is in the hands of a close corporation, who discourage individual enterprise, and through the system of
advances to farmers, keep them in a state of subjection
injurious to their interests as agriculturists." [1]

Observations on the above Cases.—The first thing which
strikes one about these cases is that they are exceptional,
comprising only five out of the thousands of articles
which are bought and sold every day.   The second point
is the distinction between the cases in which the use of
the official test or brand is voluntary, and the cases in

---

[1] See Parl. Paper, C. 3309, p. 23, 1881.

which it is compulsory.   In the former the interference
is very slight ; it is a convenience offered, not an obligation imposed, and it is consequently not open to many
of the objections which apply to a compulsory test.
Lastly, as regards the cases in which the use of the
brand   is   compulsory,   it   is   to   be   observed   that
in   the   case   of   gun-barrels,   and   of   chains   and
anchors,   the   safety   of   human   life   is   concerned,   and
not simply the advantage or convenience of the producer or consumer ; and that in the two other cases,
viz., those of compulsory hall-marking and of the Cork
butter brand, the operation of the system is eminently
unsatisfactory, and affords no legitimate precedent for
further interference of the same kind.   I am led to
make these observations, because many persons, including among them distinguished economists, have
appealed to these cases as affording precedents for
invoking the interference of the State for the purpose
of protecting purchasers to an extent, which I believe
to be mischievous.   The rule " *Caveat emptor* " is the
sound general rule, economically and .socially as well
as legally, to which no exception should be allowed
unless for strong and special reasons.   Official guaran-
tees of articles sold in the market, especially if compulsory, are objectionable on many grounds, but principally
because the keen self-interest of private purchasers is
sure on the whole to produce a higher quality and
character of goods than any official test ; and because
to teach people to buy and sell according to an official
report, instead of using their own judgment, weakens
their energy and intelligence.

Trade Marks.—There is the less reason for further
extension of the official branding or testing system, now

that the State has, by legislation on the subject of trade marks, recognised to the full the importance of giving to manufacturers the means of making their own brands known and of protecting them from imitation. A *quasi* property in trade marks has long been recognised by the courts of law, and the remedies for infringement of trade marks were strengthened by statute in 1862 (25 & 26 Vict. ch. 88).   But the Legislature has carried the protection of trade marks much further by the Act 38 & 39 Vict. ch. 91, under which every manufacturer and trader has the right of registering his trade mark in a public office.   This registration gives him at once a *primâ facie* exclusive right, and after five years a conclusive right, to it, and no one else at home or abroad can then use or imitate it.   Its value to him depends on the goodness of his wares and the character they bear; and the system thus acts, not as an official brand must generally do, as a premium on mediocrity, but as a stimulus to special excellence.   The statutes above mentioned are supplemented by a provision in the Customs Act, 39 & 40 Vict. ch. 42, which prevents foreign goods with English trade marks from being imported into the United Kingdom.

Adulteration Acts.—Another form of interference in favour of purchasers is to be found in the Adulteration Act, 38 & 39 Vict. ch. 63, amended in 1869.   Under these acts it is a crime to mix any ingredients with articles of food so as to make them injurious to health, or to mix any ingredient with drugs so as to affect their quality injuriously, or to sell any articles of food or drugs so mixed, or to sell any article of food or drug which is not what the purchaser asks for.   If mixed with innocent ingredients the article must be labelled accordingly.

Local authorities are empowered to appoint analysts, and purchasers of food or drugs may take them to the public analyst to be examined. Public officers may obtain samples of food or drugs and submit them to the analyst. If the analysis proves the article to be such as the act forbids, the seller is subject to a penalty. Tea is to be examined on importation by an analyst appointed by the Customs, and if unfit for food to be destroyed.

This act embodies two different principles. The one is the prohibition of the sale of articles which are injurious to health, an object which has always been considered to call for special intervention, as will appear more fully in the next chapter; the other is the principle that a seller is bound to perform his contract in good faith, and to use no concealment. When an adulterated article is injurious to health the sale is *ipso facto* criminal. When an article is adulterated, but the adulteration is not injurious to health, the seller is bound to give ample notice of what he is selling. In this there is no official interference with freedom of contract as generally understood. The further provision for examination by a public analyst only provides a summary and easy mode of enforcing both branches of the act by means of a trustworthy expert, instead of having recourse to the expensive and inefficient remedy afforded by the common law in the shape of a trial before a jury assisted by what is known as scientific evidence.

To similar principles may be referred an act of last session, 45 & 46 Vict. ch. 41, s. 6, which requires adulterated coffee to be so labelled as to give notice to the purchaser of the substances with which it is adulterated.

Also an Act of 1866 (29 Vict. ch. 37) which requires sacks of hops to be marked with the name of the grower, the quantity and the year of growth ; and prohibits the packing of foreign hops in English bags.

Also a clause in the Customs Acts, which requires foreign plate to be marked with the letter F.

Also an Act of 1869, 32 & 33 Vict. ch. 112, amended in 1878, which makes it a criminal offence to kill or dye agricultural seeds, or to sell seeds so killed or dyed with intent to defraud purchasers.

Of some of these provisions it may perhaps be doubted whether they are, as is generally professed, for the protection of consumers, or for the protection of certain classes of producers.

CHAPTER XVII.

INTERFERENCE OF THE STATE WITH SPECIAL TRADES IN ORDER TO SECURE HEALTH AND SAFETY.

In the cases we have been considering, the inter-vention of the State is supposed to have for its principal object or one of its principal objects the protection of the purchaser in the performance of the contract. It interferes to see that he gets what he bargained for. But there is another large class of cases in which the State intervenes with a view to some object outside the contract, generally for purposes connected with health or the protection of human life, and in some cases, for the purpose of preventing serious annoyance.

In some cases it is for the purpose of protecting the workman or others employed in the business, as is the case with the Factory Acts, the Mining Acts, and a large part of the Merchant Shipping Acts. These cases have been already discussed by Mr. Stanley Jevons in his *Treatise on the Relation of the State to Labour*, and I therefore need only make a general reference to them. In a second class of cases the persons to be protected are the purchasers and users of some commodity or convenience, such as passengers by ship or railway, who are or are supposed to be unable to protect themselves.   In a third class of cases the persons to be protected are persons outside the special business concerned, who may be injured in life or health or otherwise prejudiced by the manner in which it is carried on.   The different cases however run into one another, and it will be sufficient to mention them shortly under the heads of the subject-matter with which they are concerned without distinguishing too curiously the special classes who are to be protected.

The principle of interference for the purpose of securing life, health, and freedom from annoyance is well known to the common law.   For private injury arising from culpable negligence on the part of a trader there is a remedy by civil action for damages, and often also a further remedy by criminal proceedings.   For everything in the nature of a public nuisance—a word of very wide and ill-defined meaning—there are also remedies at common law.   But these common law remedies have been found insufficient, and modern legislation has surrounded a number of trades with special regulations and conditions, and has often enforced these conditions by the appointment of inspectors whose business it is to see that the law is enforced.   It cannot be too often repeated that these remedies, though generally stated in the statutes which create them to be cumulative, and to be an addition to those of the common law, are and must be really in substitution for those remedies.   When the State prescribes the way in which a thing is to be done—still more, when by its own officer it certifies that the thing has been done, it cannot afterwards hold the doer liable for the consequences. If, therefore, the precaution ordered is unwise or ineffectual it may prove to have an effect to the contrary of what was intended. Ships may be sent to the bottom by Act of Parliament, and no one is to blame. Although this is no sound argument against interference where interference is shown to be both wise and necessary, it is an argument which, independently of any consideration for the interests of the trade which is interfered with, should make philanthropy cautious in the selection of those regulations and inspections which it so constantly and passionately advocates.

There is one form of State interference which is open to none of these objections, and which has been considerably extended of late, viz., that of public inquiry into a casualty or death, with the view of ascertaining the causes. The effect of such an inquiry is twofold. If the casualty has happened from culpable neglect or default, it brings home the fault to the culpable party, and often exposes him to actions for damages or other proceedings. If the accident has arisen from preventible causes it helps the parties interested to provide against similar causes in the future. Such inquiries are founded on the same principle as the old coroners' inquests. They have been applied in different forms to outbreaks of disease ; to ships ; to railways ; to mines ; and in the last session to boiler explosions ; and will probably still further receive application.

I proceed to give shortly a list of some of the principal instances of the special State interferences with trade, to which this chapter relates.

Ships.—To State interference with shipping for purposes of safety, I need only refer here, as it is more fully described above in Chapter XIII.

Railways.—In the case of railways, the permanent

works and all their adjuncts must be inspected and reported to be safe by an officer of the Board of Trade before the line can be opened for passenger traffic. After the line is opened the Board of Trade have power to inspect it, and report upon it. The Board of Trade have also various powers with respect to the crossing of railways, including a power with respect to railways authorised since 1863 to require a bridge to be substituted for a level crossing. They may give power to take land to prevent immediate danger, and may require screens to be erected to prevent horses from being frightened.

The Board of Trade also require and publish returns of all accidents, and have the power of inquiring into the causes of all accidents on railways, &c. This important power is constantly and regularly exercised, and the results are made public.

Tramways.—Before a tramway can be opened for passenger traffic it must be inspected by an officer of the Board of Trade and certified to be fit for use. The Board of Trade have also power to allow or disallow bye-laws regulating the use of a tramway; and, in the case of proposals to use steam on tramways, to grant licenses under such conditions as may be needed for public safety.

Hackney Carriages are subject to license, inspection, and regulation, both in London and in other towns. The case is worthy of special notice because it is one, and perhaps the only one, in which, there being no monopoly or privilege, the State, in regulating the service, also fixes the price. This point has been adverted to above, in Chapter VIII.

Unwholesome Food.—Public officers are authorised to inspect and examine all articles of food exposed for sale, and if they appear to them to be unwholesome or unfit to be used as food, may seize them, and take the articles and their owner before a Court of Summary Jurisdiction, which may order the articles to be destroyed and may fine the owners.

The adulteration of food and drugs has been referred to in the previous chapter.

Offensive Trades.—Certain trades which are offensive to the neighbourhood—such as those of bone-boilers and tallow-melters—cannot be established without the consent of the local authority, and if already established may be suppressed, if they are proved to be a serious nuisance.[1]

Gas.—The acts relating to gas contain various stringent provisions against allowing the waste products of gas manufacture to become a nuisance by fouling air or water.[2] The case deserves special notice, because the waste products of gas have, by recent discoveries, become the raw materials of dyeing stuffs, creosote, artificial manures, and other products, the making and sale of which promises to be, if it is not already, as profitable as the manufacture of gas itself. The secondary effect of the statutory provisions which prevent them from being thrown into and polluting our rivers has been to quicken invention, and promote profitable trade.

Electric Lighting.—By a statute passed last Session (45 & 46 Vict. ch. 56), provision is made that in each license or order for electric lighting regulations shall be introduced to prevent danger by fire, electric shock, or

[1] Public Health Act, 1875, §§ 116 to 119.
[2] Public Health Act, 1875, §§ 112 to 116.

otherwise ; and the Board of Trade have, in addition, power to make such further regulations as they think necessary for these purposes.

Chemical Works.—By the 44 & 45 Vict. ch. 37, 1881, it is provided that in order to prevent the escape of noxious gases, which are a nuisance to the neighbourhood, works for manufacturing alkali, sulphuric acid, nitric acid, chemical manure, sulphate or muriate of ammonia, and bleaching powder or liquor, must be registered, and must be inspected by a Government officer to see that the act is obeyed. In certain cases specific rules and conditions are made for the conduct of the manufacture, and in other cases it is made obligatory on the manufacturer, under severe penalties, to use the best practical means to prevent the escape of noxious gases.

Smoke.—Under the Public Health Act 1875, ss. 91, 92, furnaces in manufactories which do not consume their own smoke, and chimneys, not being the chimneys of private dwelling-houses, which send forth black smoke, are declared to be nuisances, and local authorities are empowered and required to abate them.

Explosives. — By the Act 38 Vict. ch. 17, 1875, very elaborate provisions have been made for regulating, and in some cases preventing altogether, the manufacture, storage, carriage, and sale of gunpowder and other explosives. The administration is in the hands of the Home Secretary, aided in certain cases by the Board of Trade, and also by local authorities. Provision is made for inquiries into accidents. The object is, of course, the public safety.

Buildings.—Under the Public Health Act, ss. 155 to 160, local authorities have the power to determine the line of frontage of houses which are re-built; and to regulate the width of new streets, the structure of new buildings, the space which is to surround them, and their drainage.

Powers for similar purposes are given to the local authorities in London so that no one can add to his house without the leave of an official surveyor.

Lodging-houses.—By the Public Health Act 1875, ss. 71 to 90, the letting of certain cellar dwellings is prohibited altogether, and local authorities are required to keep a register of, and to inspect and regulate, all common lodging-houses. They are to fix the number of lodgers, and to see that cleanliness, ventilation, and water supply are provided, and that precautions are taken against the spread of disease.

It has already been noticed in Chapter X. that municipal authorities have in certain cases power to pull down bad houses and supply workmen's dwellings themselves.

Bakehouses.—By 26 & 27 Vict. ch. 40, 1863, specific regulations are made for the cleanliness of bakehouses, and for separating them from sleeping places, and local authorities are required to enforce these regulations.

Slaughter-houses.—Under an Act of 1847 (10 & 11 Vict. ch. 34, s. 135, and 125 to 131) these must be registered and licensed by the local authority, and are subject to inspection and to regulations to be made by the local authority for the purpose of preventing cruelty and preserving cleanliness.

Public-houses.—It is needless and impracticable in a treatise of this nature to do more than refer to the well known and much debated laws by which the State has interfered with this great trade. It is a very remarkable case, because the State, anxious as it has no doubt been to promote public health and morality, has managed by its interference to create a gigantic vested interest partaking of the character of a monopoly, whose political influence and power is such as to render it a matter of the greatest difficulty either to introduce freedom of trade, or to impose further regulations and restrictions in the interest of the public health and morality.

Theatres.—Under an Act of 1843, (6 & 7 Vict. c. 68), every theatre in London or in any place where the Queen resides must be licensed by the Lord Chamberlain, and in other places by the Justices of the Peace. Rules may be made for the regulation of the theatre, and in case of the breach of the rules, or other misconduct, the license may be withdrawn and the theatre closed.

All plays must be submitted to the Lord Chamberlain for his approval before they are acted, and he may forbid any play to be acted which he thinks injurious to good manners, decorum, or the public peace.

In effect the Censorship over the stage is complete and absolute.

Cattle.—By various acts, and now by 41 & 42 Vict. ch. 74, 1878, known as the Contagious Diseases (Animals) Act, very stringent regulations have been made to prevent the spread of disease in cattle. The following is an official description of its purport :—

First, in regard to home stock, the act deals most stringently with disease in the homesteads, and seeks to confine infection to those centres, leaving the movement of animals in the country generally as free from restriction as possible. Animals found to be

M

affected with pleuro-pneumonia or foot and mouth
disease, or swine fever, in a market, railway station,
grazing park, or other like place, or during transit, are
to be detained ; but those which have been herded with
them are *free to move* as if no disease had been detected.

Secondly, in regard to the foreign animals trade, the
act proceeds on the assumption that all imported stock
is to be slaughtered at the place of landing, leaving to
the Privy Council a certain amount of discretionary
power, guarded, however, by strict conditions, to prohibit importation altogether from some countries, and
to permit it under modified restrictions from others.

General Observations.—The above does not pretend to
be a complete or exhaustive list of State interferences
of this description, and if it were complete to-day, it
would be incomplete to-morrow, for new circumstances
constantly call for fresh interference. There is in it,
however, enough to show that the State will and does
interfere whenever a strong enough case is made out.

As to the result of this kind of interference it is
difficult, if not impossible, to give a general or an absolute answer. In many of the cases mentioned, probably
in most, the interference has no doubt to some extent,
directly or indirectly, effected its purpose. " To call
public attention to an evil is in itself a remedy," was
the observation of a wise minister ; and the passing of
a law may have a powerful effect even if not actually
enforced. But I believe that it would, in most of the
above cases, be extremely difficult to ascertain positively
by examination of the results how far the interference
has been successful in effecting the objects for which it
was intended.   Our present statistics are of little value

where the causes of the facts which they record are numerous and complicated. *Post hoc* for *propter hoc* is the commonest of fallacies, and as the statistics are generally collected by the same hands which administer the remedies, there is abundant room for self-deception. I have tried very hard to ascertain the results of the laws which for half my life I have been helping to administer, and I am quite unable to say with any degree of accuracy what amount of evil has been prevented by them. Still more difficult is it to say whether, with the evil, any and what amount of good has been prevented. These observations are made not for the purpose of preventing interference, but of showing the need for caution.

The ever-increasing complexity of our society; the size of our towns; the congregation of many men in small spaces; the vastness of our industrial organisations, and the consequent difficulties of exercising free individual action, and of enforcing individual liability; the progress of knowledge, pointing out dangers in common life which in former times were not apprehended and which can often be successfully attacked only by some form of common action such as the State alone can supply; the progress of invention, which brings with it, not perhaps greater danger to life, but danger to life on a larger scale; all these point to necessities for increasing intervention on the part of governments, central or municipal. But on the whole, the danger at present appears to me to lie in the direction of too much restriction, not of too much freedom. Legislative interference cannot be too cautiously applied. There is the great difficulty of making any general rule which shall apply to the infinite variety of human dealings and circumstances, even in the best known and commonest trades ; and there is the still greater difficulty of foreseeing future circumstances, and of altering rules as the ever-changing circumstances of all trades require.   If, as is frequently the case, an attempt is made to meet these difficulties by giving a power of discretionary interference to a public department, the effect is to give the department absolute and arbitrary power.   It must be remembered that in these technical matters the collective wisdom of a government department in a special case, means generally the wisdom of the particular inspector or officer who has examined the case.   In proportion as the action is transferred from him to the higher officers of the department, the special knowledge of the case diminishes also. A member of the cabinet cannot be expected to know much about the strength of a particular boiler, or the efficiency of a given safety-valve.   These objections to intervention impress themselves strongly on those who, like myself, have been engaged in central administration.   They are met to some extent by transferring the responsibility from the central government to local authorities ; and, as will be seen from the foregoing references, recent legislation has taken a strong turn in this direction.   That it has done so is well, not only for the matter in hand, but for the general political future of the country, which depends so largely on the soundness and vigour of our local institutions.

There is, however, another objection which is not met by any transfer of the power of intervention to local bodies ; the objection, namely, that it may unduly restrict individual freedom.   This is a subject on which it is difficult to avoid misunderstanding.   The sacred name of freedom has been largely used of late by those who were not formerly its friends, to uphold a very different cause, viz. the sanctity of vested interests. With such advocacy of freedom I have no sympathy. But that there is a real danger to true freedom, and to the sort of character which it creates, in the constant demand for Government interference, I cannot doubt. Treat grown men or women as incapable of judging and acting for themselves, and you go far to make them incapable. Our daily life is beginning already to be hedged round by inspections, regulations, and prohibitions. The coming democracy has much of promise in it; but one of its failings is impatience. It cannot bear to see an evil slowly cure itself, which can, as it imagines, be cured at once by the use of its own overwhelming force. It is passionately benevolent, and passionately fond of power. To preserve individual liberty in trade, as in other matters, from the impatient action of philanthropy, will probably be one of the great difficulties of the future.

CHAPTER XVIII.

ALL taxation has a tendency to reduce trade; it diminishes the means of buying and selling, and converts what might be used for the purpose of production and exchange, to purposes which are immediately unproductive. But it is scarcely necessary to say that trade reaps the full benefit of a judicious Government expenditure on law, on police, on education, and also from expenditure on the army and navy, so far as these are properly used for purposes of defence and protection.

But this is not the place to discuss the general effect of taxation, or the nature and merits of different taxes, and the indirect modes in which they affect trade. It will be sufficient here to point out what are the taxes levied by our Government which directly affect buying and selling. They consist, in the first place, of taxes on commodities, which raise the price to the seller, and which thus contract sales, and reduce consumption. Of these there are—

1. *Taxes on commodities imported from abroad.*

Tea produced in 1881 . . . . £3,974,000

Coffee 189,000

Cocoa	£52,000
Dried fruits	517,000
Spirits	4,223,000
Wine . . . . : .	1,336,000
Tobacco	8,838,000
Other articles	650,000

2. *On commodities produced in the country.*

Spirits produced in 1881	£14,273,000
Beer	8,530,000
Gold and silver plate	68,000

In the second place there are license duties on the following trades : sellers of beer, wine, and spirits ; distillers, brewers, keepers of refreshment houses, dealers in game, auctioneers, pedlars, pawnbrokers, patent medicine sellers, dealers in gold and silver plate, playing card makers, tobacco manufacturers and dealers, vinegar makers, which produced in 1881 upwards of £2,000,000. These must of course be recouped out of the profits of their respective businesses, and therefore add to the price of the articles sold.

In the third place there are stamp duties on commercial transactions, which *pro tanto* reduce the profits and increase price. These are levied—

On Bills and Notes, producing in 1881 . .	£756,000
On Receipts and Cheques	889,000
On Marine Insurances	141,000

In the fourth place there is the railway passenger duty, which in 1882 amounted to £798,333. It is the anomalous remnant of the taxes on various means of locomotion which formerly existed, and it is open to objection on account of the exemption from it of what are called cheap parliamentary trains, and the difficulties which arise from that exemption. But it is in most cases a tax not so much on locomotion, or on passengers, as on railway dividends.

It is to be observed with respect to these taxes that, putting aside alcoholic liquors, the articles of food now taxed are tea, coffee, and cocoa ; and that tobacco, and alcoholic liquors, both of which may be considered luxuries, produced together in 1881 £37,000,000, or not far from half of the £85,882,000 which constituted our whole national income.

None of the above taxes are levied on what are usually known as the raw materials of our ordinary manufacture; nor are any of them, unless it be the excise on alcoholic liquors, taxes which necessitate the vexatious interference of the exciseman in the processes of manufacture. Nor are any of these taxes of such a nature as to protect English manufacturers against foreign competition. When a tax is levied on an imported commodity, such as alcoholic liquors, a similar tax is levied on the same articles produced in the country. Nor are any of the taxes on imported articles intentionally differential as between one foreign country and another. In the case of wine, the present alcoholic standard is thought to give advantages to the light wines of France over the stronger wines of Spain, Portugal, and the colonies. But this differential effect was not intended, and will probably soon be remedied.

Finally, the whole tariff is one of great simplicity, when compared with most foreign and colonial tariffs.

As regards local taxation, there is little in this

country which can be said to be a direct burden on trade.

By far the greater part of the expense of local government is paid for by direct rates upon property.[1] The whole sum raised by local taxation in 1880 was £31,043,100, and of this £25,926,943 was raised by rates. Of the remainder, £437,946 consisted of the duties on coal, wine, and corn, levied by the City of London, which are applied for metropolitan improvements; and the remainder, £4,678,211, consisted of rents of property belonging to local authorities and tolls. Of these tolls all, or almost all, are special payments for special services rendered to the special trades which pay them, such as tolls for the use of markets, bridges, ferries, and roads; and light, pilotage, and harbour dues. If the amount of the receipts for special services rendered and for rents, which are not given separately in the return, were deducted from the sum of £4,678,211, the sum remaining would be very small, and the whole amount received in the shape of taxes on articles bought and sold must come out of this sum. In fact, including the £437,946 of London dues, the taxes levied on trade by local authorities for general purposes, do not probably amount to half a million.

Many persons would be glad to see the taxes on tea, coffee, and cocoa, abolished. But we may fairly say that our taxation, both general and local, has been so arranged as to throw no undue burdens on trade.

[1] See the return of local taxation contained in Parliamentary Paper 112, 1882.

CHAPTER XIX.

WE have hitherto been considering the relations of the state to trade in times of peace; but the state has also special relations to trade in time of war, or apprehended war. In considering these we must bear in mind what has been said in an earlier chapter concerning the trading position of England amongst other nations. We have incomparably the largest stake in the commerce of the world; we have the largest quantity of foreign investments, most of which are made by means of the export of goods, and the profit on which returns to us by the import of goods; we have the largest quantity of property liable to capture and destruction at sea; we have a merchant navy, one of our most important industries, which is more than equal to the merchant navies of all other nations. It is therefore our interest, far more than that of any other nation, to try to make the laws of war such that they shall do as little harm as possible to peaceful trade.

We have, it is true, a war navy more powerful than that of any other nation, and greater means than any other nation of making it still more powerful; and I fully believe that our superiority in this respect is as

great as it ever was. But great as our power
at sea unquestionably is, its ability to injure an
enemy by destroying his trade is limited ; and its
ability to defend our own merchant shipping at sea
is limited also. Add to this that our investments
are so widespread and all-pervading that we should
never know whether in destroying an enemy's property we were not destroying our own. It was said
that the timber which we destroyed in Russia during
the Crimean war belonged to English merchants. Had
we gone to war with the United States about the
Trent or the *Alabama*, and made prize of ships sailing
from the East to New York under the Stars and
Stripes, we should have been destroying the security
for advances made by London merchants. Modern
trade is so universal, so complicated, and so connected,
that the loss of one trading nation is the loss of all ; and
as we are the greatest traders, and the greatest capitalists, we should generally and probably suffer most by
any great injury to trade. It is important not to lose
sight of these facts, because there are those amongst
us who regret any restriction of the belligerent rights
which were formerly exercised by ourselves and others,
and who think that a full restoration and stringent
exercise of those rights would help to maintain our
trading superiority. Bearing then these general observations in mind, let us consider the various cases in
which war affects trade.

Restrictions on Exports and Imports.—First then there
is the case where we apprehend danger either at home
or abroad, with or without actual war. To meet such
cases the Government has power under the Act 39 and
40 Vict. ch. 36, §§ 43 & 138, to forbid the importation

of arms, ammunition, gunpowder, and other goods, and also to prohibit the exportation of arms, ammunition, stores, and food.

Foreign Enlistment Act.—Secondly, there is the case when we are at peace and other nations are at war. In this case the State does not interfere with ordinary trade. With the exception mentioned below, Englishmen are free to trade as they please with either belligerent, subject to the chance of capture by the other belligerent if they break blockade or carry contraband of war. But the English Foreign Enlistment Act (1870), forbids them to build, or equip, or despatch a ship which is to be used in the naval service of either of the belligerents; or to add to the equipment of any ship of war of either of the belligerents (meaning by equipment, the furnishing of arms, ammunition, provisions, or stores of any kind). These prohibitions are enforced by penalties, by stringent powers of seizure, and by forfeiture. This act, which amends and strengthens the act previously in force, was passed after the American civil war, and in consequence of the difficulties which had arisen in the case of the *Alabama* and other similar ships. Coupled with other enactments it enables our Government to carry into effect the substance of the celebrated three rules adopted in the Washington Treaty, which in general terms bind each nation to use due diligence to prevent the fitting out, arming, or equipping, or departure, of any vessel which is intended or adapted to carry on war against a power with which it is at peace, and not to allow either belligerent to make use of its ports as the base of naval operations against the other. These rules, as is well known, were adopted by England and the United States, and were to have been proposed to other nations as part of the general maritime law of the world. It is deeply to be regretted that preposterous claims for compensation on the one side, legal mismanagement on the other, and general bad temper between the nations, prevented the Alabama Treaty—in itself one of the noblest and most successful attempts ever yet made to put an end to national quarrels by conciliatory means—from being crowned by a settlement of a disputed point of international law, which would have been an immense gain to the trade of the world generally, and especially to that of this country. It is obvious from what has been said before, that no nation has so great an interest as we, with our enormous property afloat, have in circumscribing the operations of hostile cruisers. We have numerous ports ourselves all round the globe at which our own cruisers can refit and equip. Other nations, with whom we might go to war, would not be so well off, and would depend for their powers of carrying on operations against our trades on the facilities given to them for obtaining coal and other stores in neutral ports. To limit such facilities is of the utmost importance to us, and any loss we might suffer by being prevented, when neutrals ourselves, from supplying stores to belligerents, would be a trifle in comparison. It is much to be desired that the three rules, or some rules embodying the same principles in better and clearer language, should be revived on some fitting occasion.

Blockade, Contraband of War, and Maritime Capture.—Thirdly, there is the case where we are at war ourselves. When this is the case British subjects are not allowed to trade with the enemy, or with the enemy's subjects.

But when we are at war, it is not so much the action of our own state which affects our trade, as the laws and principles which the governments of all civilised nations have recognised as regulating the mode in which one enemy may seek to destroy the commerce of the other. The three principal weapons which international law recognises as proper to be employed by a belligerent for this purpose, are blockade, seizure of contraband of war, and maritime capture. The two former are employed against the trade of the enemy carried on under a neutral flag. Under the law of maritime capture an enemy seizes and makes prize of the ship which carries the flag of the other belligerent, however and wherever employed, so long as she is not within the territorial jurisdiction of some neutral country.

By the law of maritime blockade, either belligerent may declare certain ports or part of the coasts of the other belligerent to be in a state of blockade, and if this declaration is supported by a sufficient blockading force, may capture any neutral ship which attempts to carry on trade with the blockaded ports. As a weapon of offence against English trade, blockade is not likely to be efficient so long as we retain our naval superiority and are able to drive away a blockading force. As a weapon of offence in our own hands it is likely to be of less value than it formerly was, because the facility of transport by railway throughout the whole of the continents of Europe and North America enables goods imported and exported through neutral or distant ports, which are unaffected by the blockade, to be carried to any part of the continents, and thus makes the blockade of a limited portion of the coast ineffectual.

Under the laws relating to contraband of war, an enemy may seize arms and munitions of war and stores which are to be used for warlike purposes when found under a neutral flag and intended for the service of the other belligerent, and may make prize of the ship. But this weapon, whether in our own hands or in that of our enemy, is likely to be a less efficient weapon than it formerly was, because coal and iron will be the most important of the articles which may be treated as contraband of war; and these being, as the lawyers say, *ancipitis usûs*, and needed by all nations for purposes of peace as well as of war, it will be very difficult, when they are found under a neutral flag, to fix the carriers of them with a warlike intention or destination.

The most important however, of these laws, is that of maritime capture. Under this law a belligerent has at sea a recognised right—which he does not possess on land—of taking and appropriating the private property of his enemy's subjects. This right has been much altered and limited by the Treaty of Paris. That treaty effected two great changes. It provided that the flag should cover the goods—that is, that an enemy's cargo carried in a neutral ship shall not be liable to capture. This doctrine has since been always acted on, and though the Americans were not parties to the treaty, it will no doubt be recognised by all nations as the maritime law of the civilised world. The second change was that privateers—that is, private persons cruising for their own profit, under licences from their own government—should no longer be allowed to make captures. By this provision the United States refused to be bound, unless on the condition, which was refused by us, that private property at sea should be exempt from capture altogether.

The result of the law of maritime capture, as it now stands, upon ourselves, is as follows:

Regarding maritime capture as a weapon of offence in our own hands, we shall be able to injure the merchant navy of our enemy, but not to destroy his trade, which will be carried on safely under a neutral flag. Regarded as a weapon of offence in our enemy's hands it will not enable him to destroy our trade, which may, like his own, be carried on under a neutral flag, but it will enable him to capture our merchant ships, which are not only more numerous and valuable than those of any other nation, but more numerous and valuable than those of all other nations put together. We shall not be able to protect them, as formerly, by convoy, for speed is of the essence of modern trade, and traffic will speedily desert ships which have to wait for convoy. Nor would convoy be effectual against fast steam cruisers. Our fastest ocean steamers will probably save themselves from capture by their own speed, but the bulk of our trade is carried on in seven or eight knot steamers, which will fall an easy prey to fast armed vessels. The result will be that premiums of insurance on English ships will rise and become ruinous, and our ships will be transferred to some foreign neutral flag, perhaps never to return. We shall then, under this law of maritime capture, be able to injure or destroy our enemy's merchant navy, and he will in most cases be able to cripple ours; but in this, as we have far more to lose than he has, we shall be the greatest sufferers.

It is impossible to discuss this subject here as its

importance deserves. But in a treatise on the relations
of the State to trade, it would be wrong to omit all
notice of a danger impending over an important branch
of our trade, which it may be in the power of the state
by successful diplomacy to remove.

It appears to me that it is deeply to our interest to
do what the Americans and others have heretofore in
vain asked us to do, viz., to extend still further than
has yet been done the principle of exempting private
property at sea from being seized or destroyed by
an enemy.

Trade and Conquest.—There is another aspect of the
relations of the State to trade in connection with its
foreign relations, which suggests still more serious
reflections. English trade is found in every quarter of
the globe, among savage and half-civilised, as well as
among civilised nations. It is found in the shape of
cargoes exchanged under the protection of the English
flag, of investments by Englishmen in the industrial
enterprises of the foreign countries, and of money lent
to foreign governments, the profits and interest of
which come back to us in the shape of goods carried
in British ships. These ships and their cargoes, these
investments of British capital, the State is called upon
to protect. Now all these operations are praiseworthy,
useful, and desirable in themselves, and if fairly and
properly conducted may carry civilisation into the waste
parts of the earth. It is the privilege of honourable
trade that, like mercy, it is twice blessed; it blesseth)
him that gives and him that takes; each of its dealings
is of necessity a benefit to both parties. But traders
and speculators are not always the most scrupulous of
mankind. Their dealings with savage and half-civilised

N

nations too often betray sharp practice, sometimes violence and wrong. The persons who carry on our trade on the outskirts of civilisation are not distinguished by a special appreciation of the rights of others, nor are the speculators who are attracted by the enormous profits to be made by precarious investments in half civilised countries, people in whose hands we should desire to place the fortunes or reputation of our country. When a difficulty arises between ourselves and one of the weaker nations, these are the persons whose voice is most loudly raised for acts of violence, of aggression, or of revenge. Our merchant navy, we are told, began its career with piracy and slave-dealing, and in some of the practices which we are now trying to repress amongst the isles of the Pacific, is still to be found a taint of its original vice. Our dealings in the far East, and elsewhere, have not always been such as would do credit to an honest merchant. The consequences have too often been repudiation, ill-will, and violent revenge. The state is then called in to protect its trade with the cannon and the bayonet, and we end with conquering where we began with buying and selling. It would be interesting to examine how many of our wars and conquests have had their origin in what ought to have been peaceful trade. For good or for evil we owe India to a trading company. Our wars in China arose out of our trade, and we should not now be in Egypt, but for our investments in that country, and our interest as traders in the Canal. Every vantage point in the map of the world becomes a port of call for English ships, and is garrisoned by an English force; the bounds of empire are extended, and subject nations are annexed. To those who reflect with Mr.

Gladstone [1] that our power, our prosperity, our empire, depend upon the character, vigour, and capacity of the people who inhabit these islands, and that this people is only thirty-five millions in number, it may well be doubted whether, in undertaking to manage such a large proportion of the world, we are not taking upon ourselves more than we are able to perform, and whether the demands which our trade thus indirectly makes upon our population do not constitute a serious drawback to the wealth and power which it brings us.   It is a reflection which ought at any rate to inspire hesitation, caution, and moderation, when we are called upon as a nation to undertake fresh risks and fresh responsibilities on behalf of our ubiquitous commerce.

[1] See his article on "Aggression in Egypt," in the *Nineteenth Century* of June, 1877.

CHAPTER XX.

WE have thus seen that the State maintains order, without which trade would be impossible; that it enforces trading contracts, and at the same time provides that their obligation shall not continue too long or become oppressive; that it determines the measures of quantity and value in which contracts are made, and supplies, though not at its own cost, the medium of exchange; that it repudiates monopoly, unless when necessary to reward invention; that it generally leaves buyers and sellers to fix their own prices; that where monopoly is inevitable it regulates price and conditions, and sometimes undertakes the supply itself; that it repudiates any attempt, by means of protective duties, or otherwise, to prevent buyers from buying what they want to buy, or to compel them to buy what they do not want to buy; that it does not hesitate to interfere with trade when it appears to be necessary to do so in order to protect life and health; that it levies a part of the general revenue of the nation upon the exchange of commodities, in return for which it gives to trade, in peace, the benefits of security from violence, of law, and of various organised modes of action without which it could not exist ; that in time of war between other nations, it enforces certain restrictions on trade for the purpose of maintaining peace ; and that when it is at war itself, it gives to trade all the protection it can, and in so doing often takes upon itself serious liabilities.

Under this system, the chief feature of which is as much individual freedom as is consistent with the welfare of an organised society, and the performance of self-imposed obligations, British trade has grown to be such as the world has never seen before. The State has given protection, and has established forms and modes of action. But its chief praise in relation to trade has been that it has left as much scope as possible to the free energy and self-interest of its people.

THE END.